My Big Fun
First Grade
Workbook

1st Grade Workbook
Math, Language Arts,
Science Activities to Support
First Grade Skills

Want Free Extra Goodies for Your Student?

Email us at: info@homerunpress.com

Title the email "My Big Fun First Grade Workbook" and we'll send some extra worksheets your way!

We create our workbooks with love and great care.
For any issues with your workbook, such as printing errors, typos, faulty binding, or something else,
please do not hesitate to contact us at: info@homerunpress.com
We will make sure you get a replacement copy immediately.

THANK YOU!

Home Run Press, LLC 1603 Capitol Ave. Suite 310 A551 Cheyenne, WY 82001 USA
info@homerunpress.com   www.homerunpress.com

First published in the USA 2020.   ISBN 9781952368325

Table of Contents

Table of Contents

Table of Contents

Hi. I'm Sunny. For me, everything is an adventure. I am ready to try anything, take chances, see what happens - and help you try, too! I like to think I'm confident, caring and have an open mind. I will cheer for your success and encourage everyone! I'm ready to be a really good friend!

I've got a problem. Well, I've always got a problem. And I don't like it. It makes me cranky, and grumpy, impatient and the truth is, I got a bad attitude. There. I said it. I admit it. And the reason I feel this way? Math! I don't get it and it bums me out. Grrrr!

Not trying to brag, but I am the smartest Brainer that ever lived - and I'm a brilliant shade of blue. That's why they call me Smarty. I love to solve problems and I'm always happy to explain how things work - to help any Brainer out there! To me, work is fun, and math is a blast!

I scare easily. Like, even just a little …Boo! Oh wow, I've scared myself! Anyway, they call me Pickles because I turn a little green when I get panicky. Especially with new stuff. Eek! And big complicated problems. Really any problem. Eek! There, I did it again.

Hi! Name's Pepper. I have what you call a positive outlook. I just think being alive is exciting! And you know something? By being friendly, kind and maybe even wise, you can have a pretty awesome day every day on this amazing planet.

A famous movie star once said, "I want to be alone." Well, I do too! I'm best when I'm dreaming, thinking, and in my own world. And so, I resist! Yes, I resist anything new, and only do things my way or quit. The rest of the Brainers have math, but I'd rather have a headache and complain. Or pout.

1. <u>Read</u>.

Earth is home to billions of animals, birds, plants, and people. People, animals, and plants need clean air to breathe and live. Air is made up of oxygen, nitrogen, carbon dioxide, and other gases. There is water in the air, too. Water makes clouds, rain, snow, and fog. Air around the earth is called the atmosphere.

2. According to the text people and animals need air to

A) breathe   B) live   C) breathe and live

3. Air is made up of

_____

_____

4. <u>What word from the text</u> means *you must have it because it is very important?* _____

5. As used in the text, <u>which word</u> could be used instead of *clean?*

A) easy   B) fresh   C) good

1. <u>Read.</u>

The Moon looks as big as the Sun. It is made of solid rock, and it is rather close to us. The Sun is shining on the Moon, and it looks like it is **glowing**. Earth is rotating around the Sun while the Moon is rotating around Earth. There are great plains, hills, mountains, and craters on the Moon.

2. <u>What part of speech</u> is the word *moon* as used in the text?

a) Noun   b) Adjective   c) Verb   d) Adverb

3. According to the text the Moon

A) looks huge;

B) looks bigger than Earth;

C) looks smaller than the Sun;

D) looks as big as the Sun.

4. As used in the text, <u>which word</u> could be used instead of **glowing**?

A) dull   B) colorful

C) dark   C) bright

1. <u>Read</u>.

Does the Sun rise in the morning? No, it doesn't! The earth turns itself around every twenty-four hours like a spinning ball. At sunrise, the part of the earth is turning towards the Sun. This part has a day. The weather may be cloudy and rainy, but above the clouds, the Sun is always shining! The other part is turning away from the Sun. Their sky is dark, and they have night.

2. <u>Circle</u> TRUE or FALSE to the following statements.

a) TRUE   FALSE

The Earth turns around Mars like a spinning ball.

b) TRUE   FALSE

When the weather is cloudy and rainy, the Sun is not shining.

c) TRUE   FALSE

The Earth turns itself around every 24 hours.

1. Read.

A day is the length of time it takes for the earth to spin around its axis. There are 24 hours in a day. A week equals seven days. One month is the length of time it takes for the Moon to rotate around the earth. There are 28, 29, 30, or 31 days in a month. A year is how long it takes for the earth to rotate around the Sun. There are 365 days in a year.

2. According to the text a day

A) is how long it takes to orbit the Moon;

B) is how long it takes to orbit the Sun;

C) is how long it takes to make one full spin of the earth.

3. The Moon rotates around the earth in

A) one day   B) one week   C) one month

4. What word from the text means *being the same in quantity?* _____

www.homerunpress.com

1. <u>Read.</u>

Why do we have seasons on the earth? The earth moves around the Sun. It takes a year from start to finish. In December, the northern part of the earth is tilted away from the Sun. This part gets less of the Sun's rays. It has winter. The southern half has summer. In six months, the northern half of the earth is tilted toward the Sun. It has summer. The southern part has winter.

2. The phrase **moves around the Sun** as used in the text refers to:

A) the Sun;

B) Mars;

C) the earth.

3. The word *northern* as used in the text means

A) opposite of summer   B) winter

C) situated on the north   D) summer

4. What word from the text means *the coldest season of the year*? _____

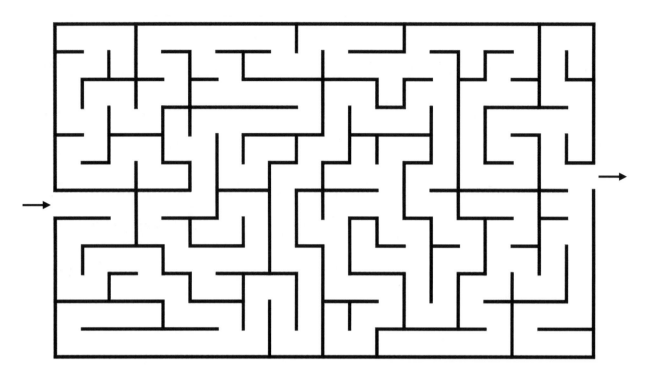

1. <u>Find</u> and <u>circle</u> or <u>cross out</u> the words.

F	S	T	X	W	D	R	H	A	E	
J	N	Y	B	Z	E	M	C	A	N	
G	N	P	A	W	A	R	A	R	O	
A	W	M	S	W	O	B	N	T	Y	
L	M	N	U	S	L	U	O	N	N	
L	A	A	S	C	E	A	T	U	A	
T	S	O	M	L	A	A	H	X	T	
K	Z	V	N	L	Q	D	E	W	V	
A	F	T	E	R	M	D	R	U	M	
L	V	D	N	K	T	A	B	L	W	

AFTER

ALL

ABOUT

ACROSS

ALMOST

ALWAYS

ANOTHER

ANYONE

ASK

ANSWER

www.homerunpress.com

1. <u>Read.</u>

People affect the earth in both good and bad ways. All of us make a lot of waste. If the oil spills into the rivers or ocean, this can kill thousands of sea creatures and birds. Villages, cities, and towns throw away a lot of waste into the rivers and lakes. Polluted water can harm people, birds, animals, and plants.

2. <u>Circle</u> the word that does rhyme with the first word in each line.

Words that rhyme end with the same arrangement of letters:

h<u>ouse</u> – m<u>ouse</u>; r<u>ight</u> - n<u>ight</u>

creature

A) feature   B) warfire   C) teacher

throw

A) so   B) know   C) threw

waste

A) based   B) chased   C) taste

1. <u>Read</u>.

How can we reduce the bad effects? We can reuse some clothes. We can recycle some materials. The glass waste can be used to make new glass or glass bottles. The waste plastic can be used to make new plastic things. The waste paper can be used to make new paper.

2. <u>Add</u> a question mark to each question.

A question mark (?) is a form of punctuation that comes at the end of a sentence to indicate that a question has been asked.

Words that can be used to ask a question: how, when, what, which, where, why, are, is, was, were.

<u>Why</u> is it important to recycle plastic__

<u>How</u> does the plastic get into the sea__

<u>Do</u> people and animals need clean air__

<u>Where</u> do plants take water__

<u>How</u> can you protect the earth__

<u>Who</u> pollute fresh water__

www.homerunpress.com

1. Read.

Air contains different gases. People, birds, and animals breathe in oxygen from the air. We need oxygen to live. People breathe out carbon dioxide. Green plants take in carbon dioxide from the air. They return oxygen to the air. This is the way people and plants help each other.

2. As used in the text, which word could be used instead of *contains*?

A) divides   B) has

C) adds   C) is

3. What do people breathe in?

A) gas   B) atmosphere

C) water   D) oxygen

4. What do plants breathe in?

A) gas   B) carbon dioxide

C) water   D) oxygen

5. What word from the text means *to work with someone to make something easier*? _____

1. <u>Read.</u>

Are you scared of skeletons? People and some animals have a skeleton in their bodies. The skeleton is the reason why you can stand. Skeletons are made of very hard and strong bones and joints. When we grow and get bigger, a skeleton grows, too. A skeleton protects the body shape and the organs from the inside. We have more than two hundred bones in our skeletons.

2. According to the text,

<u>which statement</u> is correct?

A) skeletons are made up of bones;

B) skeletons are made up of muscles;

C) skeletons are scary;

D) skeletons support our bodies from the inside .

3. When we grow,

A) a skeleton changes   B)   we get smaller

C) a skeleton moves   C)   a skeleton grows

1. <u>Read</u>.

What makes my heart beat? When I sit still and watch cartoons, my heart beats slower. When I am running a race with my friend, my heart beats faster. My teacher says it happens because my body needs more oxygen. My brain makes my heart beat automatically. It never stops beating, even when I am asleep. When my heart beats or pumps, it pushes blood to every part of my body and back again.

2. <u>Write</u> the numbers 1 to 4 to show the correct order in which events occurred in the story.

___ It never stops beating.

___ My heart beats slower.

___ What makes my heart beat?

___ My brain makes my heart beat automatically.

3. <u>Which statement</u> is correct?

A) The blood delivers oxygen to every part of my body.

B) I have to remember to make my heart beat.

1. Read.

Ears help me hear. I hear my mom calling me to dinner. I hear my brother honking for me to get out of the way. Sounds reach my ears, and messages are sent to the brain. The brain tells me what the sound means. It happens very fast.

2. Circle one of the four words that means almost the same as the first word.

Synonyms are words that have similar meanings.

tell	A) open	B) say	C) move	D) yell
call	A) shout	B) whisper	C) do	D) slow
fast	A) quiet	B) quick	C) aloud	D) slow
reach	A) leave	B) start	C) get	D) fail

3. Circle one of the four words that means the opposite of the first word.

Antonyms are words that have opposite meanings.

send	A) post	B) receive	C) mail	D) make
slow	A) good	B) huge	C) fast	D) easy
get	A) give	B) win	C) buy	D) grab

 www.homerunpress.com

1. Read.

There is one long backbone inside a snake's body. It is made up of many small bones. A snake moves by making its skin crawl. When a snake moves, the muscles bend, and the edges of the scales grip the ground. That is why a snake moves faster on a rough surface. It cannot push its body on smooth ground. It moves in curves.

2. According to the text, which statement is correct?

A) A snake's body is long.

B) A snake's body is smooth.

C) A snake's body is made
of many long backbones.

D) A snake's backbone is
made of many small bones.

3. A snake moves

A) in a straight line

B) on Monday

C) in curves

C) in circles

1. Read.

Glass is transparent. That means you can see through it. Glass is clear, and it lets the light shine through. We use glass for windows. It lets sunlight into the room. Eyeglasses use special lenses to help a person with eye problems see better. Some eyeglasses help people see far things clearly. Other glasses help people see near things clearly.

2. As used in the text, which word could be used instead of *transparent*?

A) fresh   B) clear

C) white   C) open

3. What do people use glass for?

A) walls   B) windows

C) toys   D) trees

4. According to the text eyeglasses help people

A) tell the time   B) see things clearly

C) see things at night   D) make shadows

1. <u>Read</u>.

When autumn comes, the leaves change color. They turn yellow, gold, red, orange, and brown. It's getting colder. Trees find it difficult to get water from the ground. So the leaves dry out and drop to the ground. The twigs and branches are bare. Some trees do not lose their leaves. Pine trees have thick needles that help keep the trees from losing water. That means they are evergreens because their leaves, or needles, are always green.

2. The purpose of this text is to

A) inform   B) persuade   C) entertain

3. <u>Circle</u> the words that could describe the color of the leaves in the fall.

black   yellow   purple   red   orange   brown

4. <u>Why</u> do some trees stay green?

A) they have strong leaves B) they are very old

C) the leaves are thick   D) their needles are thick

1. <u>Read</u>.

Who makes a rainbow? Sunlight is made up of lots of different colors. When it's raining, the sun shines through the tiny raindrops in the air. The water makes the sunlight spread into different colors. The colors appear in the same order: red, orange, yellow, green, blue, indigo, and violet. On a sunny day, you can make a rainbow! Turn on the sprinkler and see a rainbow in the spray!

2. <u>Which word</u> could be used instead of *appear* as it is used in the text?

A) are seen   B) show   C) end

3. The word *sunny* has a similar meaning to

A) rainy   B) bright   C) dull

4. The text provides

A) facts   B) warnings

C) explanations   C) amusements

5. <u>What word from the text</u> means *to create*?

_____

1. <u>Read</u>. <u>Write</u> **a** or **an** before the nouns.

Use a before words that begin with a consonant sound (a <u>p</u>ig, a <u>w</u>ig, a <u>t</u>ree, a <u>c</u>ake, a <u>b</u>one.)

Use an before words that begin with a vowel sound (an <u>i</u>nch, an <u>a</u>pple, an <u>o</u>wl, an <u>e</u>gg.)

Bears use ___ <u>c</u>ave, ___ <u>t</u>ree, or ___ <u>h</u>ole for ___ <u>b</u>ed to sleep in.

___ <u>b</u>ear likes sweet-tasting things.

The sweetest treat for ___ <u>b</u>ear is honey.

When ___ <u>b</u>ear finds ___ <u>h</u>ive, it uses its claw to get the honey.

I have seen ___ <u>b</u>rown bear.

I have seen ___ <u>w</u>hite bear.

___ <u>p</u>olar bear lives on the sea ice.

I have never seen ___ <u>o</u>range bear.

1. <u>Read</u>. <u>Write</u> the word family for each group.

Word family is a group of words that has the same combination of letters and a similar sound.

- _____

a f<u>ake</u> sn<u>ake</u> in a l<u>ake</u>

t<u>ake</u> and sh<u>ake</u> a r<u>ake</u>

b<u>ake</u> a chocolate c<u>ake</u>

- _____

n<u>ame</u> your g<u>ame</u>

a fr<u>ame</u> is not the s<u>ame</u>

c<u>ame</u> to t<u>ame</u> a tiger

- _____

a b<u>ee</u> on a tr<u>ee</u>

s<u>ee</u> thr<u>ee</u>

agr<u>ee</u> and be fr<u>ee</u>

- _____

a l<u>ate</u> d<u>ate</u>

a pl<u>ate</u> in a g<u>ate</u>

too l<u>ate</u> to sk<u>ate</u>

- _____

a qu<u>ail</u> with a t<u>ail</u>

a sn<u>ail</u> on a tr<u>ail</u>

a n<u>ail</u> in a m<u>ail</u>

- _____

a w<u>et</u> n<u>et</u>

find a v<u>et</u> for a p<u>et</u>

I m<u>et</u> a j<u>et</u>

www.homerunpress.com

1. <u>Read</u>. <u>Find</u> and <u>write</u> the missing word that makes the best sense in each sentence. <u>Capitalize</u> the first word of a sentence.

there were _____ than 2000 gods in Ancient Egypt.

a. more   b. as   c. much

the Egyptians started to _____ pyramids more than four thousands years ago.

a. need   b. build   c. move

it took _____ of workers and more than 2 million blocks to make the Great Pyramid.

a. tens   b. ones   c. thousands

the largest statue in the _____ world was the Sphinx.

a. modern   b. ancient   c. far

it had the _____ of a lion and the head of a man.

a. body   b. leg   c. ears

1. <u>Find</u> and <u>circle</u> or <u>cross out</u> the words.

```
Y M A B V B V E O I I U
P E O L E R S D Z R A P
T O L F S U U E T I R W
K N O L A O H K B R O N
R R E C O T L S A E U E
E E E R R W J A C H N V
N B T A E D F V K T D E
I O E A O F O G R O U P
L R I G W P F O A N W Y
E X A M P L E I G A A W
N U Y A I R Q G D W U Y
Z N H P X K D V A A R I
```

WRITE	WAY	WATER	YELLOW
AIR	AROUND	ANOTHER	ALSO
ASKED	BACK	BEFORE	BOOK
BECAUSE	EARTH	GROUP	GIRL
DIFFERENT	GOOD	EVEN	EXAMPLE

www.homerunpress.com

1. <u>Read</u>. <u>Underline</u> the nouns.

A noun is a word that identifies a person, place, or thing.

The <u>dinosaurs</u> lived on <u>Earth</u> for <u>millions</u> of <u>years</u>.

Dinosaur means terrible lizard.

Some dinosaurs were small.

Many dinosaurs were huge.

Some dinosaurs had horns and bony armor.

Dinosaurs laid their eggs on land.

Some dinosaurs ate only plants.

There were tiny and huge flying dinosaurs.

Dinosaurs had small brains and lungs to breathe air.

1. <u>Underline</u> four nouns for each picture.

red	eat	worm
cloud	leaf	sweet
smiling	green	watermelon

owl	sleep	tree
black	circle	round
big	fly	twig

snake	scary	pretty
long	spot	flower
tongue	crawl	brown

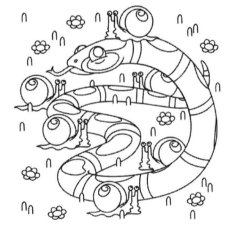

fast	squirrel	tall
high	funny	autumn
jump	tail	grass

www.homerunpress.com

1. <u>Read</u>. <u>Circle</u> the adjectives and <u>underline</u> the nouns they describe.

A noun is a word that identifies a person, place, or thing.

An adjective is a word that describes a noun or pronoun.

Brontosaurus was a (huge strong) <u>dinosaur</u>.

Tyrannosaurus rex was the fiercest dinosaur on the earth.

Pterosaur was a flying dinosaur which looked like an enormous bat.

Quetzalcoatlus was the largest animal ever to fly.

Diatryma was a tall bird. It had a huge bill.

Indricotherium was a gigantic rhino. It weighed more than a modern elephant.

1. <u>Underline</u> five adjectives for each picture.

hot	eat	banana
happy	leaf	tall
blue	green	cloud

strong	kangaroo	grass
key	long	fast
fresh	air	high

lemon	yellow	lion
happy	find	huge
hungry	eyes	large

mouse	small	tail
cute	big	short
look	ask	grey

www.homerunpress.com

1. <u>Read</u>. <u>Circle</u> the right adjective to describe the noun.

animal

a. walk   b. do   c. white   d. purple

bird

a. bee   b. thick   c. tiny   d. easy

land

a. close   b. green   c. begin   d. plant

sea

a. blue   b. year   c. net   d. early

dinosaur

a. new   b. huge   c. about   d. south

rock

a. rainy   b. warm   c. solid   d. open

whale

a. fly   b. hot   c. wood   d. long

1. <u>Find</u> and <u>circle</u> or <u>cross out</u> the words.

```
R  E  H  T  O  M  O  A  L  D  M  E
L  Z  N  H  E  I  F  A  E  N  O  V
A  I  E  V  N  N  A  D  T  I  S  A
G  L  I  S  B  I  E  M  T  K  T  E
P  L  I  N  E  G  V  B  E  N  B  L
I  D  L  I  R  H  S  M  R  A  A  O
E  N  Z  A  H  T  U  L  S  I  N  M
H  S  L  Q  N  C  E  V  O  M  C  S
N  K  U  I  H  D  W  Y  W  K  V  N
W  C  R  O  L  E  A  R  N  O  J  I
U  I  C  C  H  X  B  E  O  V  N  W
E  M  O  H  L  Z  E  C  X  D  I  K
```

HELP	HOME	HOUSE	INSIDE
KNOW	KIND	LEAVE	LIVE
LINE	LARGE	LAND	LETTERS
LEARN	MOST	MUCH	MEANS
MAN	MOVE	MOTHER	NIGHT

 www.homerunpress.com

1. <u>Read</u>. <u>Circle</u> the verb in each sentence.

Verbs are words that show action.

A dog(is)a furry animal with four legs.

A young dog is called a puppy.

There are many kinds of dogs.

Dogs make good pets.

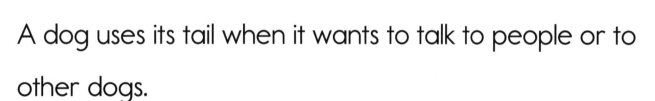

A dog uses its tail when it wants to talk to people or to

other dogs.

When a puppy wags its tail, it may want to play.

When a puppy puts its tail between its legs, it is scared.

When dogs want to play, they bark.

Some dogs bark when they get angry.

Other dogs bark when they want to tell their owner

about a stranger near the house.

1. <u>Read</u>. <u>Use</u> the the words ("try", "tried," "turns," "turn," or "turned") to write the correct verb tense for each sentence. <u>Capitalize</u> the pronoun I.

Verb tenses (past, present, future) tell if the action takes place in the past (I liked chocolate ice-cream), present (I like vanilla ice-cream), or future (I will see you tomorrow).

i usually _____ hard not to laugh when i watch

"Trolls."

i _____ hard not to laugh when i was watching

"Trolls."

i will _____ harder to read more.

The weather usually _____ colder in November.

In the fall, leaves _____ color.

My brother will _____ ten next year.

1. <u>Read</u> and <u>write</u> the correct tense of the verb. <u>Use</u> the words **present, past, or future.**

Sharks <u>are</u> heavy.

_____

If sharks <u>stop</u> swimming, they <u>will sink</u>.

_____   _____

The shark <u>looked</u> hungry.   _____

Dolphins <u>are</u> small whales.   _____

The dolphine <u>made</u> whistles and clicks.   _____

Most of dolphins <u>will live</u> in the ocean.   _____

Whales <u>live</u> in the ocean, too.   _____

The blue whale <u>is</u> the largest animal.   _____

Ichthyosaurs <u>were</u> as big as blue whales._____

When whales <u>want</u> to play, they <u>will dive</u> under a bunch of seaweed.

_____   _____

1. <u>Read</u>. <u>Circle</u> and <u>write in</u> the missing word.

Homophones are words that are spelled differently but sound the same.

A _____ (bear/bare)'s color helps it to find food.

Squirrels save nuts so that they will have food when the trees are _____ (bear/bare).

A _____ (board/bored) bear likes to catch fish.

Sometimes a bear sits on a _____ (board/bored) and waits for fish to swim by.

A _____ (be/bee) makes its honey from flowers.

So the hive and honey can _____ (be/bee) sweet for the bears.

A spider makes webs to trap insects _____ (for/four) food.

_____ (For/Four) flies were caught in the trap.

 www.homerunpress.com

1. <u>Read</u>. <u>Change</u> two words in each sentence to a contraction and <u>rewrite</u> the sentence. <u>Use</u> the contractions from the Choice Box.

Contractions are shortened words, where you use an apostrophe (') in place of the missing letters.

can't	doesn't	you're	it's

When it is very cold, clouds are cold, too.

_____

_____

The Sun does not go anywhere at night.

_____

_____

You cannot feel the earth moving because you are moving with it.

_____

_____

1. <u>Read</u>. <u>Draw</u> a line from the contraction to the two words for which it stands.

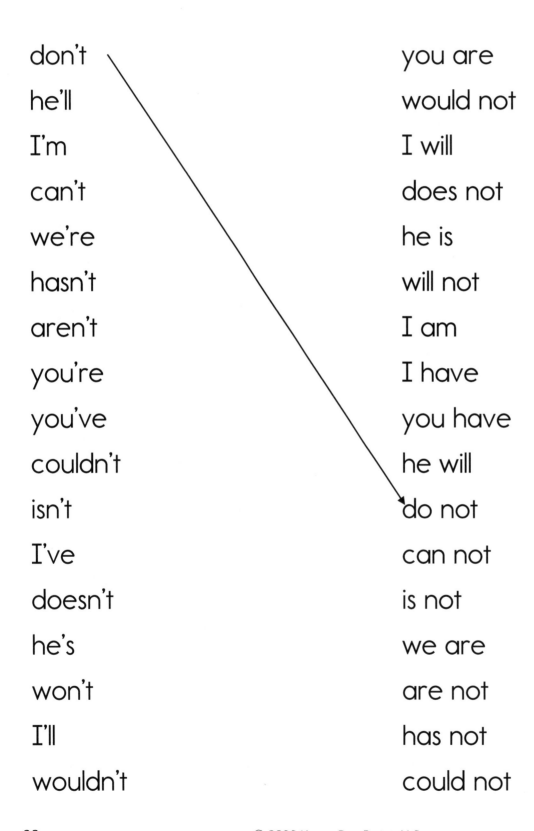

don't	you are
he'll	would not
I'm	I will
can't	does not
we're	he is
hasn't	will not
aren't	I am
you're	I have
you've	you have
couldn't	he will
isn't	do not
I've	can not
doesn't	is not
he's	we are
won't	are not
I'll	has not
wouldn't	could not

1. Find and circle or cross out the words.

```
S  B  T  S  T  E  E  T  Y  Q  G  H
N  O  A  H  S  O  O  Z  L  U  A  C
S  W  M  O  G  G  O  O  L  E  W  T
B  E  H  E  E  U  O  K  A  S  A  A
I  T  C  T  T  H  O  F  E  T  L  W
L  R  H  O  C  H  E  H  R  I  K  B
A  E  S  S  N  P  I  T  T  O  E  A
R  S  O  N  G  D  F  N  A  N  D  R
D  E  T  R  A  T  S  Y  G  T  I  U
P  S  E  E  M  E  D  H  T  V  S  N
Y  R  O  T  S  L  G  G  E  G  A  I
S  Z  O  Q  I  Z  Q  R  S  M  R  H
```

RIVER	RUN	QUESTION	REALLY
SCHOOL	STARTED	SAW	STORY
SEA	STATE	SOMETHING	SEEMED
SONG	SECOND	THOUGHT	TOOK
WATCH	WALKED	TOGETHER	THOSE

1. <u>Use</u> each fragment to create and write a complete sentence. <u>Read</u> each sentence.

A complete sentence is a group of words that form a complete thought.

I am kind and helpful.

A sentence fragment is a group of words that do not form a complete thought.

I am kind. And helpful.

I catch a cold. From germs.

_____

These germs. Are called viruses.

_____

Viruses are tiny complicated molecules. That float in

the air.

_____

_____

 www.homerunpress.com

1. <u>Read</u>. <u>Use</u> the letters in each word below to make two or more smaller words with at least two letters (against: sit, sat, gain, gas, ant, sing, sign, at, in, an, etc.).

cold

cod, _____

healthy

heal, _____

washing

sign, _____

sickness

neck, _____

sneezing

nine, _____

coughing

chin, _____

1. <u>Read</u>. <u>Write</u> in the missing words from the Choice Box and complete each sentence with a question mark.

An interrogative sentence has a question. We use a question mark ("?") at the end of an interrogative sentence. Words like what, where, why, *and* how *can often start questions.*

Do *you* <u>know</u> my favorite dinosaur?

do	do	do	does	is	do	does	do

Why _____ the spoon get hot when I stir my hot

tea___

Why _____ soap make bubbles in the bathtub___

How _____ sharks breathe___

What _____ down in the ground___

Why _____ train whistle___

How _____ a caterpillar turn into a butterfly___

Where _____ Christmas trees come from___

Where _____ rabbits live___

1. <u>Read</u> the words. <u>Write</u> the word that is a whole thing and then, the words that are parts of the whole.

baby   boy   kids   girl

Whole _____

Parts _____   _____   _____

books   library   librarian   magazines

Whole _____

Parts _____   _____   _____

student   teacher   classroom   school

Whole _____

Parts _____   _____   _____

read   write   add   learn

Whole _____

Parts _____   _____   _____

left   forward   direction   right

Whole _____

Parts _____   _____   _____

1. <u>Rewrite</u> the words in order from highest to lowest in size or degree.

nice, great, bad   _____

better, good, best _____

2. <u>Unscramble</u> a compound word.

A compound word is formed when two words are joined together to make a new word.

ridb + eohus

_____
a box to provide for a bird

ni + iesd

_____
the inner part of something

ands + obx

_____
kids play with sand in it

otne + koob

_____
you write notes in it

www.homerunpress.com

1. <u>Look</u> at the words and think about how they are related. <u>Find</u> the missing word in the list and <u>write</u> it.

back is to **front** as **closed** is to _____

      a. open   b. add   c. stop

runner is to **runs** as **worker** is to _____

      a. plays   b. works   c. talks

2. <u>Use</u> the code to find out the word.

w = ß   r = Ō   a = £   y = Â   h = Ø   o = ∞

ß Ø Â _____   ß Ō ∞ t e _____

ß Ø £ t _____   Ø £ Ō d _____

1. <u>Find</u> and <u>circle</u> or <u>cross out</u> the words.

```
X P Y H S T H K W R L Y
C A A A F G P Z N H T R
S E M G U Y W O D I Y E
P E N O E S E L I B H V
N R R C X H R R N N N T
M H O D G O U Y D U T S
T T Z F W W T B B W S R
S H O U L D C N L S O N
N R U T L H I F P K U S
P L A Y N B P E G O N W
E Q L A K A L C Y E D E
I Q G Z B L W S E T E Q
```

PICTURE	PLAY	POINT	PAGE
SOUND	SAY	SHOW	SET
SAME	STUDY	SHOULD	SPELL
THINK	THROUGH	THREE	TURN
WORLD	WANT	WHY	VERY

     www.homerunpress.com

1. <u>Read</u>. <u>Write</u> the best synonym from the choice box.

Synonyms are words that have the same or almost the same meaning.

guys	stone	go	learn	watch
far	Mom	mad	pay	washed
say	make	big	gate	nap	happy

move _____   talk _____

sleep _____   clean _____

glad _____   large _____

spend _____   door _____

miles _____   men _____

angry _____   build _____

study _____   rock _____

mother _____   look _____

1. <u>Read</u>. <u>Circle</u> the best synonym in the list.

Synonyms are words that have the same or almost the same meanings.

close	a. near	b. hand	c. open
right	a. left	b. correct	c. false
paint	a. color	b. write	c. erase
cry	a. sing	b. bring	c. weep
sad	a. glad	b. unhappy	c. joy
foot	a. body	b. leg	c. run
car	a. plane	b. vehicle	c. train
glove	a. mitten	b. hat	c. shoe
children	a. boys	b. girls	c. kids
wide	a. short	b. large	c. cut
fine	a. bad	b. kind	c. great
tame	a. pet	b. strong	c. wild

 www.homerunpress.com

1. <u>Read</u>. <u>Write</u> the best antonym from the choice box.

Antonyms are words that have the opposite meanings.

night	full	glad	dirty	big	come
short	take	noise		future	near
found	light	bottom	cold		asleep

silence _____   day _____

awake _____   sad _____

past _____   far _____

top _____   clean _____

lost _____   hot _____

long _____   empty _____

little _____   heavy _____

go _____   give _____

1. <u>Read</u>. <u>Circle</u> the best antonym in the list.

Antonyms are words that have the opposite meanings.

beginning   a. start   b. opening   c. end

kind   a. cool   b. nice   c. mean

close   a. do   b. open   c. walk

seek   a. explore   b. hide   c. play

best   a. good   b. bad   c. worst

quiet   a. noisy   b. whisper   c. wild

beautiful   a. red   b. ugly   c. wonderful

big   a. huge   b. large   c. tiny

longer   a. taller   b. shorter   c. higher

catch   a. throw   b. play   c. ball

black   a. red   b. white   c. sky

1. Read. Circle the best antonym in the list.

Antonyms are words that have the opposite meanings.

sometimes	a. now	b. there	c. often
heavy	a. thin	b. big	c. light
cry	a. shout	b. laugh	c. sing
soon	a. shortly	b. late	c. now
agree	a. confirm	b. disagree	c. reply

2. Use the code to find out the word.

r = ß   e = Ō   l = £   g = Â   a = Ǿ   n = ∞

s ∞ o w _____   h Ǿ p p y _____

∞ i c Ō _____   £ i ∞ Ō _____

s m Ǿ l l _____   c ß Ō Ō p _____

£ Ǿ ß Â Ō _____   c ß Ǿ w £ _____

1. <u>Unscramble</u> the words.

sifh   terwa   cplae

_____   _____   _____

2. <u>Read</u>. <u>Circle</u> the 15 errors in the story. <u>Write</u> the corrections above each error.

Ocne upon a time a small fish lived in an wonderful place. It loved teh warm waters in spring adn the beautiful coral. Erevy morning it wos happy to oppen its eyes dan say, "Good morning!"

It used its fins lyke paddles to push through the woter. It got the oxygen from wate. It breathed through special budy parts called gills. It travelled in an group of fish called a school. They travelled like that for protection if an big fush attacked.

1. <u>Find</u> and <u>circle</u> or <u>cross out</u> the words.

```
D L U C E S H F N A C T
W A A N H T Y O O O V S
A H N Y O I Y A U O B O
D X I B R A L N W E D M
D H M T R E T D L L C L
D M A C E R V O R A A A
G I L B Y H W E R E Q L
Z Q S E N O U G H K N O
B E G I N N I N G R Y N
R E W S N A G E B O Q G
B E S T F P M C Z W G Y
R V G M P P K U S K V O
```

WORK	WHITE	ANIMALS	ADD
ALONG	ANSWER	ALWAYS	BOTH
ALMOST	BELOW	BEGINNING	BEST
BEGAN	COUNTRY	CHILDREN	CAR
CRAYON	ENOUGH	EVERY	FOOD

1. <u>Look</u> at the words and think about how they are related. <u>Find</u> the missing word in the list and write it.

stand	point	page	first

carpet is to **rug** as **dot** is to _____

word is to **letter** as **book** is to _____

out is to **in** as **sit** is to _____

light is to **heavy** as **last** is to _____

2. <u>Look</u> at the words and think about how they are related or alike. <u>Circle</u> the right letter.

whistle   **return**   **wear**

a) adjective   b) noun   c) verb

circle   **square**   **triangle**

a) direction   b) shape   c) change

cm   **ruler**   **inch**

a) add   b) geometry   c) counting

        www.homerunpress.com

1. <u>Read</u>. <u>Find</u> and <u>write</u> the missing word that makes the best sense in each sentence.

Romans _____ in Rome more than 2000 years ago.

   a. stood   b. moved   c. lived

The best _____ had glass windows.

   a. toys   b. houses   c. cars

Most kids did not go to _____.

   a. school   b. library   c. party

Children learned to write and _____.

   a. play   b. read   c. clean

Romans discovered how to _____ concrete.

   a. glue   b. stick   c. make

Romans built straight roads, _____, and tunnels where possible.

   a. bricks   b. bridges   c. stores

1. <u>Look</u> at the words and think about how they are related. <u>Find</u> the missing word in the list and <u>write</u> it.

yellow, black, brown, _____

    a. kind   b. stop   c. white

mammals, birds, reptiles, insects: _____

    a. things   b. animals   c. humans

task, problem, question: _____

    a. learn   b. play   c. sing

job, duty, effort, _____

    a. work   b. relax   c. talk

bedroom, living room, kitchen, _____

    a. home   b. company   c. study

paper   book   library

    a. school   b. store   c. playground

1. <u>Read</u>. <u>Write</u> the missing word ("far," "farther," or "further").

The word further refers to time or amount.

The legend about Sparta goes _____ back to the ancient times. Sparta had two kings. Most people were slaves. Spartans did not work at all. They dedicated themselves to becoming the greatest warriors in the world. The boys left their families at the age of 7. Girls were educated and competed in sports, too. _____ information about Spartans is available in books about ancient Greece.

The words far and farther refer to length or distance.

What distance did the kids jump? The boy jumped _____. The girl jumped _____.

1. <u>Read.</u> <u>Use</u> the letters in each word below to make two or more smaller words with at least two letters (against: sit, sat, again.)

notice _____

often _____

2. <u>Read.</u> <u>Add</u> one letter from the choice box to make a new word.

d, g, m, t

own, _____

b, h, l, s

and, _____

3. <u>Read.</u> <u>Change</u> the first letter from the choice box to make a new word.

d, f, l, m, p

nine, _____

1. <u>Look</u> at the words and <u>think</u> about how they are related or alike. <u>Circle</u> the right letter.

object   **thing**   **item**

  A. piece   B. answer   C. book

pond   **lake**   **sea**

  A. island   B. ocean   C. earth

flowers   **trees**   **bushes**

  A. alive   B. blooming   C. plants

leaves   **twigs**   **branches**

  A. trees   B. spring   C. grow

2. <u>Look</u> at the words and <u>think</u> about how they are related. <u>Continue</u> a sequence using a word from the list.

story	tomorrow	something

nothing, anything,   _____

yesterday, today,   _____

letters, words, sentences,   _____

1. Find and circle or cross out the words.

```
L A S T I M O C H L O R
F O P C L K W J L I B T
W A E K G S G D N S J S
N I M P O R T A N T E L
L K F I O T P F H L C R
F T L W L E H G E U T E
A F D I E Y I G H E Q V
C L G K F N P W I G T E
E H O F T E N O A M I N
T Z S F E V M N E T A H
H R R D Q B Q K L P Y E
M N R E T A L D R A H W
```

FEET	FACE	FAMILY	GROW
HARD	HIGH	IMPORTANT	ICE
KNOW	KEEP	LIGHT	LAST
LIFE	LIST	LATER	MIGHT
NEVER	NIGHT	OFTEN	OBJECT

www.homerunpress.com

1. Read.

When I add 3 candies and 2 candies, there are 5 candies altogether. It does not matter which way I add candies together.

3 + 2 = 5 candies

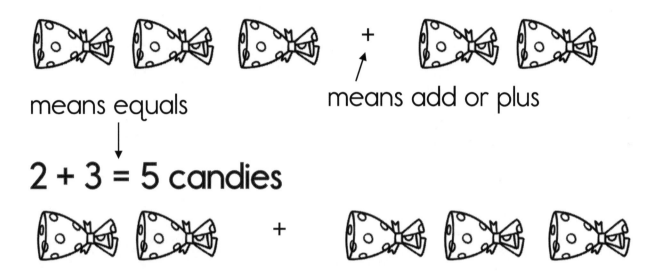

means equals

means add or plus

2 + 3 = 5 candies

I add 4 cars and 3 trucks.

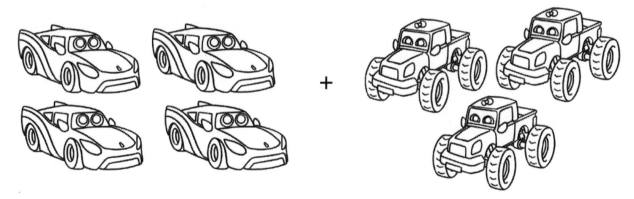

I have 4 cars and 3 trucks together. I can find the total simply by counting them all. There are 7 in all.

$$4 + 3 = 7$$

1. Read.

I use a number line to find out the answer when I add 4 and 2. First, I <u>draw</u> a line and <u>mark</u> it with numbers. I find 4 on the number line.

Start counting at 4.

I need to add 2, so I jump 2 places to the right.

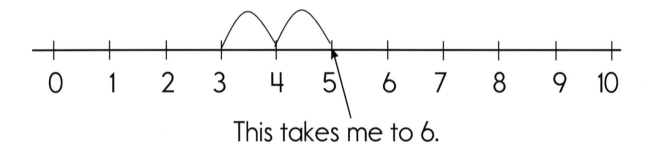

This takes me to 6.

So   4 + 2 = 6

I add 30 and 50. First, I find 30. Then, I jump 5 places to the right.

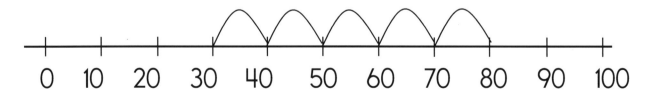

So   30 + 50 = 80

1. <u>Add</u>. Use a number line to show the jumps.

2 + 7 = ___

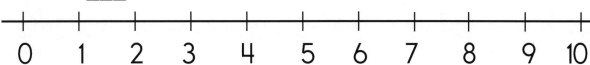

6 + 4 = ___

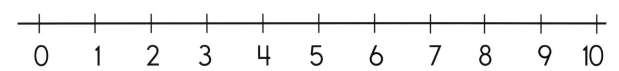

9 + 1 = ___

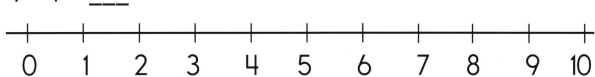

50 + 50 = ___

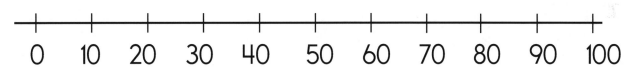

40 + 40 = ___

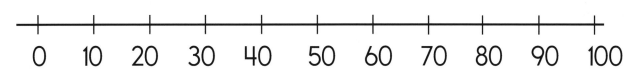

30 + 70 = ___

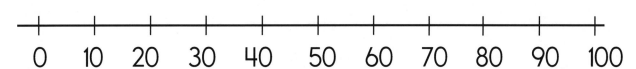

1. Read.

I like to split the adding numbers into numbers that are easier to work with. I can show my favorite strategy. T = tens, O = ones.

Step 1. Let's add 12 and 15.

```
T O   T O
1 2 + 1 5 = ___
```

Step 2. Add the tens together.

```
T O   T O   T O
1 0 + 1 0 = 2 0
```

Step 3. Add the ones together.

```
T O   T O   T O
  2 +   5 =   7
```

Step 4. Add the tens and ones to find the total.

```
T     O   T O
2 0 + 7 = 2 7
```

1. Add.

16 + 12 = 10 + 10 + 6 + 2 = ___ + ___ = ___

21 + 17 = ___ + ___ + __ + __ = ___ + ___ = ___

13 + 15 = ___ + ___ + __ + __ = ___ + ___ = ___

www.homerunpress.com

I can add numbers using column addition. Hint: Write ones under ones. Write tens under tens.

Step 1: Write the digits that have the same place value lined up one above the other.

```
tens  ones
  1     2
+ 1     5
_____
  -     -
```

Step 2: Start by adding the ones together. Add 2 ones and 5 ones: 2 + 5 = 7

Write 7 in the ones column.

```
tens  ones
  1    (2)
+ 1    (5)
_____
  -    (7)
```

Step 3: Add 1 ten and 1 ten. But I actually add 10 and 10. So the answer is:

10 + 10 = 20

I write 2 in the tens column.

```
tens  ones
 (1)    2
+(1)    5
_____
 (2)    7
```

1. <u>Add.</u>

$$
\begin{array}{r} 3 \\ + 3 \\ \hline 6 \end{array}
\qquad
\begin{array}{r} 5 \\ + 2 \\ \hline \end{array}
\qquad
\begin{array}{r} 3 \\ + 6 \\ \hline \end{array}
\qquad
\begin{array}{r} 7 \\ + 2 \\ \hline \end{array}
\qquad
\begin{array}{r} 4 \\ + 4 \\ \hline \end{array}
\qquad
\begin{array}{r} 8 \\ + 1 \\ \hline \end{array}
$$

$$
\begin{array}{r} 2 \\ + 8 \\ \hline \end{array}
\qquad
\begin{array}{r} 5 \\ + 5 \\ \hline \end{array}
\qquad
\begin{array}{r} 3 \\ + 7 \\ \hline \end{array}
\qquad
\begin{array}{r} 4 \\ + 6 \\ \hline \end{array}
\qquad
\begin{array}{r} 1 \\ + 9 \\ \hline \end{array}
\qquad
\begin{array}{r} 6 \\ + 4 \\ \hline \end{array}
$$

2. <u>Complete</u> each pair of number bonds.

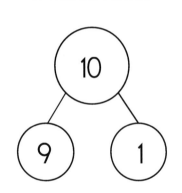

9 and 1 make 10

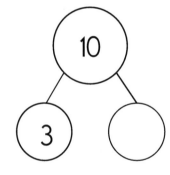

3 and __ make 10

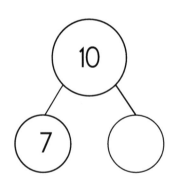

7 and __ make 10

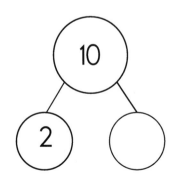

2 and __ make 10

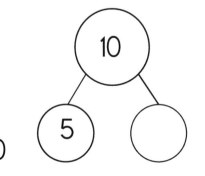

4 and __ make 10

5 and __ make 10

www.homerunpress.com

1. <u>Use</u> cupcakes to make 10. <u>Color</u> the cupcakes brown and yellow.

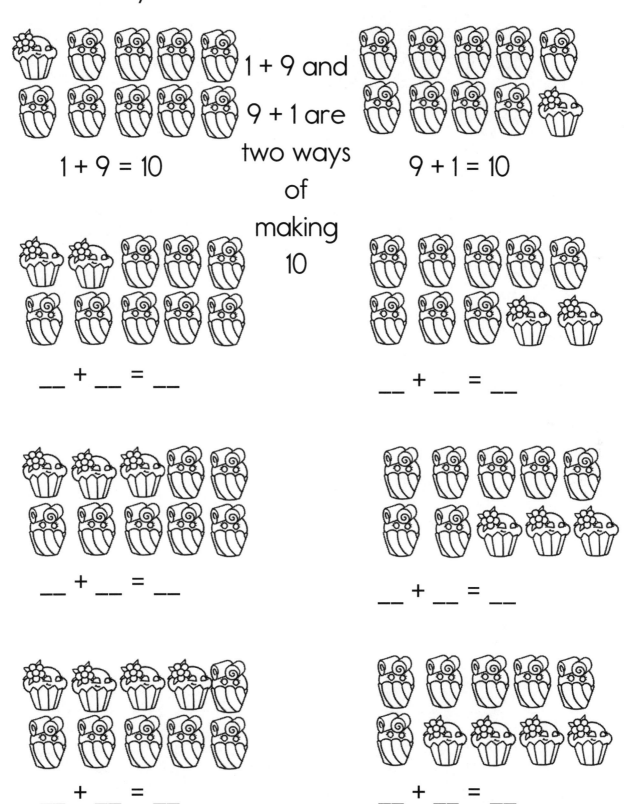

1 + 9 and 9 + 1 are two ways of making 10

1 + 9 = 10

9 + 1 = 10

__ + __ = __

__ + __ = __

__ + __ = __

__ + __ = __

__ + __ = __

__ + __ = __

1.   <u>Complete</u> each picture. When a shape is symmetrical, each half is a mirror image of the other.

Symmetry

line of symmetry

2. <u>Add.</u>

1	2	3	6	4	8
+ 7	+ 5	+ 3	+ 2	+ 1	+ 1
8					

2	1	3	2	3	6
+ 6	+ 5	+ 5	+ 2	+ 4	+ 1

     www.homerunpress.com

Subtraction is the opposite of addition. Subtraction means finding the difference between two numbers or taking away from a number. When I give 2 candies to my sister out of 3 candies that I have, how many candies are left?

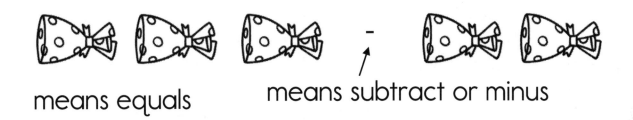

means equals   means subtract or minus

3 - 2 = 1 candy

When I subtract or take away 2 cars from the 4 cars that my brother has, he is left with 2 cars.

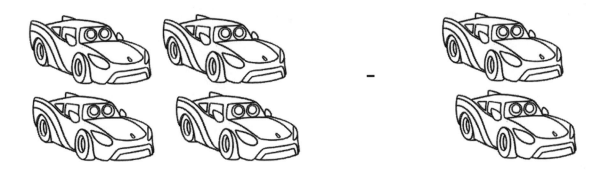

He has 4 cars and I take away 2 cars. I can find the total simply by crossing out the 2 cars from the 4 cars. There are 2 cars left. 4 - 2 = 2

1. Read.

I use a number line to find out the answer when I subtract 4 from 7. First, I draw a line and mark it with numbers. I find 7 on the number line.

Start counting at 7.

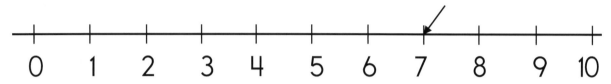

I need to take away 4, so I jump 4 places to the left.

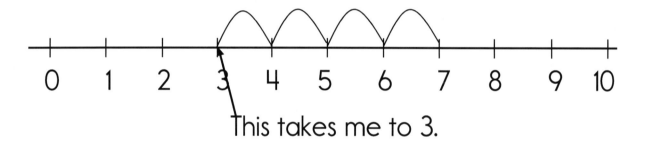

This takes me to 3.

So   7 - 4 = 3

I subtract 40 from 60. First, I find 60. Then, I jump 4 places to the left.

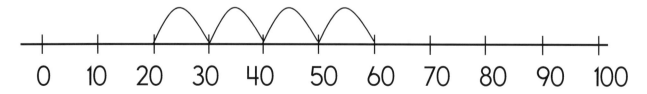

So   60 - 40 = 20

          www.homerunpress.com

1. <u>Subtract</u>. Use a number line to show the jumps.

9 - 6 = ___

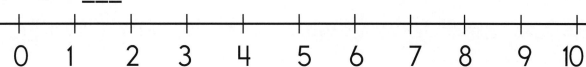

7 - 5 = ___

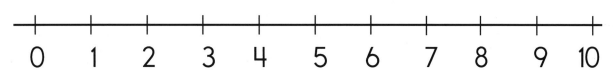

10 - 7 = ___

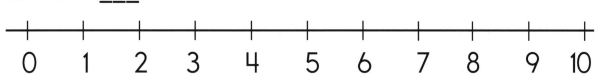

80 - 30 = ___

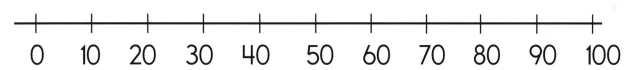

60 - 50 = ___

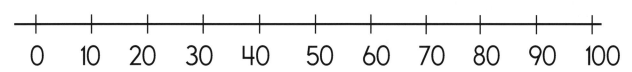

100 - 70 = ___

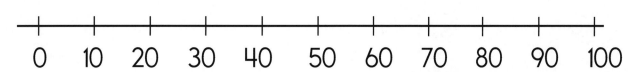

1. Read.

I like to split the numbers I subtract into numbers that are easier to work with. I can show my favorite strategy.

Step 1. Let's subtract 13 from 38.

T O T O
3 8 - 1 3 = ___

Step 2. Subtract the tens from 38.

T O T O T O
3 8 - 1 0 = 2 8

Step 3. Subtract the ones from the remaining 38.

T O T O T O
3 8 - 3 = 3 5

1. Subtract.

$5 - 1 =$ ___ $6 - 1 =$ ___ $9 - 1 =$ ___

$8 - 2 =$ ___ $4 - 2 =$ ___ $7 - 2 =$ ___

$3 - 3 =$ ___ $6 - 3 =$ ___ $8 - 3 =$ ___

$7 - 4 =$ ___ $9 - 4 =$ ___ $5 - 4 =$ ___

www.homerunpress.com

I can subtract numbers using column subtraction. Hint: Write ones under ones. Write tens under tens.

Step 1: Write the digits that have the same place value lined up one above the other.

tens	ones
2	9
- 1	3
—	—

Step 2: Subtract 3 ones from 9 ones: 9 - 3 = 6

Write 6 in the ones column.

tens	ones
2	(9)
- 1	(3)
—	(6)

Step 3: Subtract 1 ten from 2 tens:

2 - 1 = 10

I write 1 in the tens column.

tens	ones
(2)	9
- (1)	3
(1)	6

1. Subtract.

9	5	8	7	4	8
- 3	- 2	- 4	- 2	- 4	- 1
6					

8	5	5	7	9	6
- 2	- 5	- 2	- 6	- 1	- 4

2. Complete each pair of number bonds.

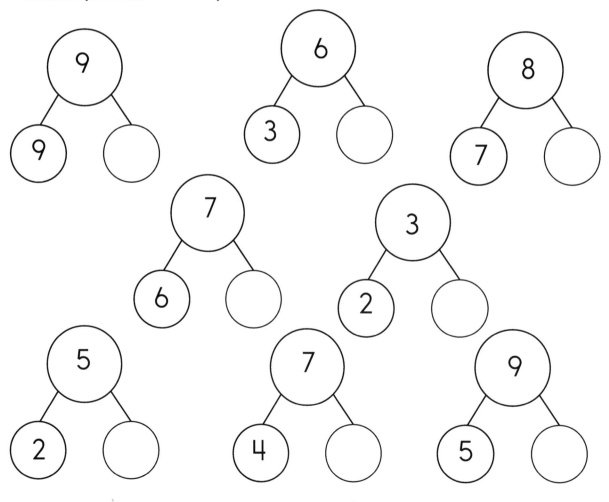

     www.homerunpress.com

1. Subtract.

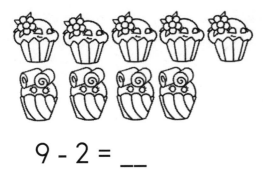

9 - 2 = __

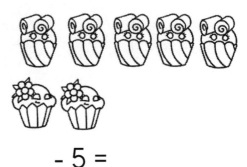

__ - 5 = __

__ - 4 = __

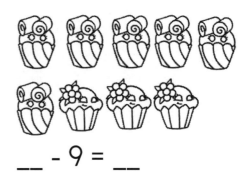

__ - 9 = __

__ - 3 = __

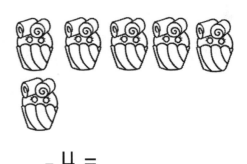

__ - 4 = __

__ - 6 = __

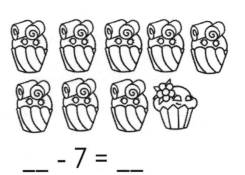

__ - 7 = __

1. If 5 cupcakes are eaten, <u>how many</u> are left?

$$10 - 5 = \underline{}$$

2. If 7 cupcakes are eaten, <u>how many</u> are left?

$$\underline{} - \underline{} = \underline{}$$

3. If 4 cupcakes are eaten, <u>how many</u> are left?

$$\underline{} - \underline{} = \underline{}$$

4. If 9 cupcakes are eaten, how many are left?

$$\underline{} - \underline{} = \underline{}$$

www.homerunpress.com

1. <u>Subtract.</u>

$$\_\_ - 5 = \_\_$$

$$\_\_ - 7 = \_\_$$

$$\_\_ - 4 = \_\_$$

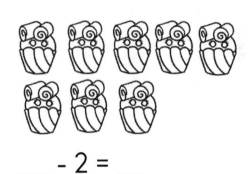

$$\_\_ - 2 = \_\_$$

2. <u>Subtract.</u>

9	8	6	6	4	8
- 7	- 5	- 3	- 1	- 3	- 4
2					

7	7	8	2	6	6
- 4	- 5	- 3	- 2	- 4	- 5

1. <u>Color</u> the flowers with the smaller number in each group.

www.homerunpress.com

1. <u>Subtract.</u>

10	10	10	10	10	10
- 3	- 5	- 6	- 2	- 4	- 1
7					

17	18	13	15	16	19
- 6	- 5	- 1	- 2	- 4	- 1

2. Complete each pair of number bonds.

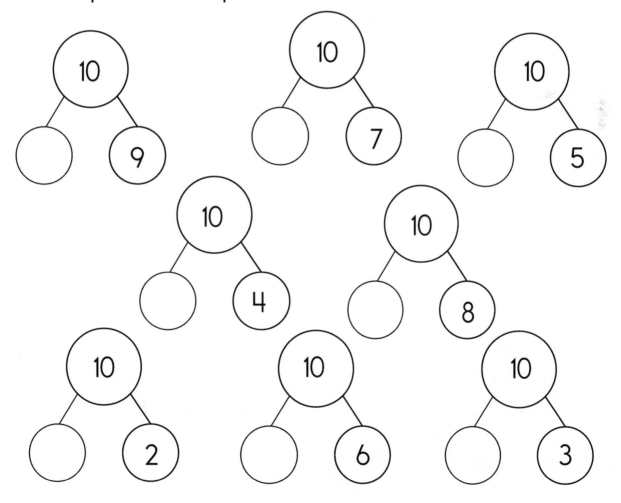

1. <u>Read</u>. <u>Write</u> how many tens. <u>Write</u> the number.

Two digit numbers are made up of tens and ones.

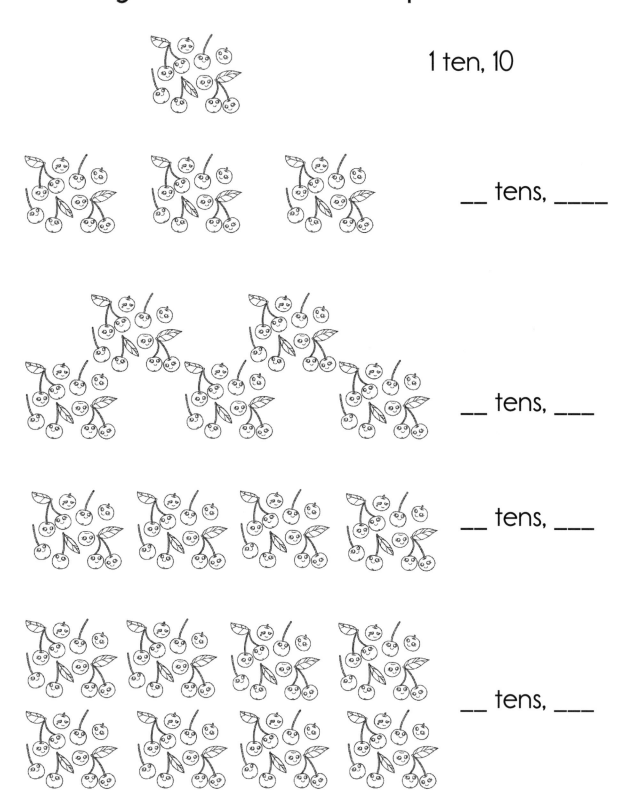

1 ten, 10

__ tens, _____

__ tens, ___

__ tens, ___

__ tens, ___

1. <u>How many</u> are there in each group?

 10

1

10 + 1 makes 11

 __

_

__ + __ makes __

 __

_

__ + __ makes __

 __

_

__ + __ makes __

 __

_

__ + __ makes __

1. <u>Add.</u>

10	10	10	10	10	10
+ 3	+ 5	+ 6	+ 2	+ 4	+ 1
13					

12	11	13	12	13	16
+ 6	+ 5	+ 5	+ 2	+ 4	+ 1

2. <u>Complete</u> each pair of number bonds.

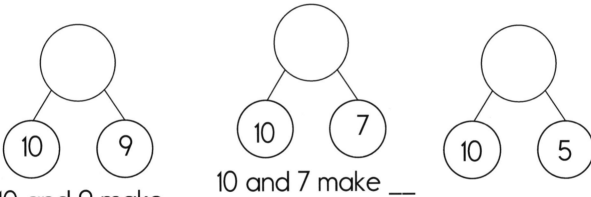

10 and 9 make __

10 and 7 make __

10 and 5 make __

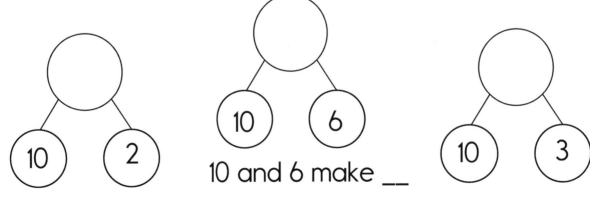

10 and 2 make __

10 and 6 make __

10 and 3 make __

www.homerunpress.com

1. <u>How many</u> are there in each group?

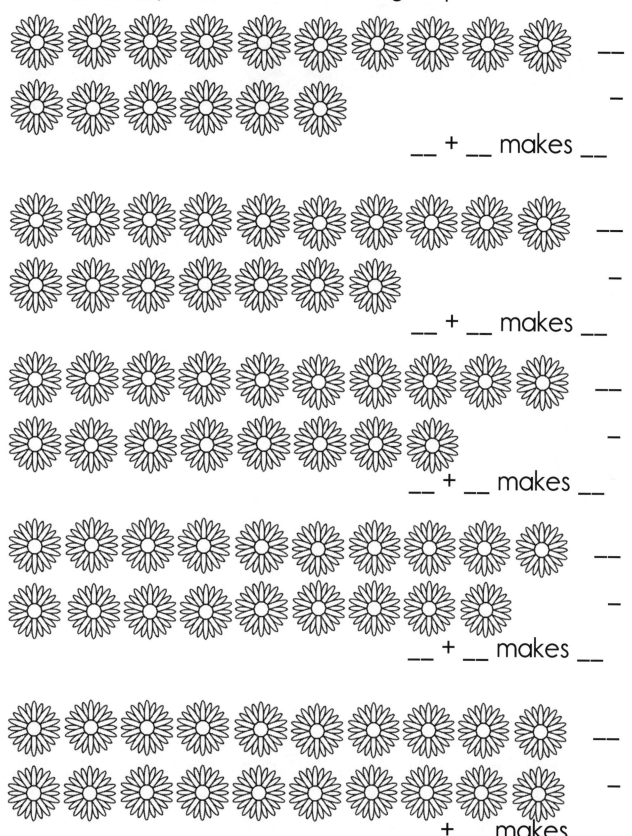

__

–

__ + __ makes __

__

–

__ + __ makes __

__

–

__ + __ makes __

__

–

__ + __ makes __

__

–

__ + __ makes __

1. Add.

20	20	30	30	30	40
+ 3	+ 5	+ 6	+ 2	+ 4	+ 1
23					

42	51	53	62	63	66
+ 6	+ 5	+ 5	+ 2	+ 4	+ 1

2. Complete each pair of number bonds.

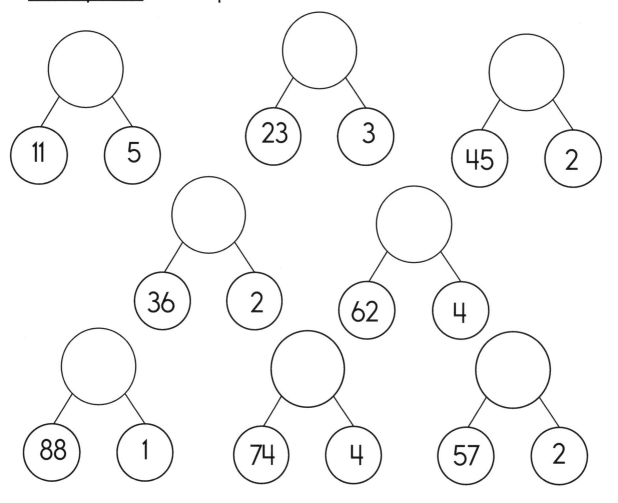

www.homerunpress.com

1. The blocks in each tower tell you how many hundreds, tens, and ones in each number. <u>Write and</u> put the numbers in order from the least to the

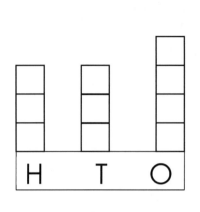 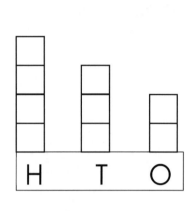 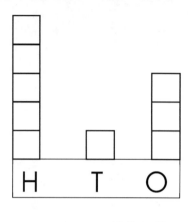

_____   _____   _____

2. <u>Write</u> the number for these.

2 tens + 5 ones = 25   1 ten + 9 ones = _____

3 tens + 0 ones = _____   5 tens + 6 ones = _____

4 tens + 9 ones = _____   6 tens + 2 ones = _____

7 tens + 0 ones = _____   8 tens + 5 ones = _____

3. <u>What</u> is the value of the digit 7 in the numbers below?

37   71   17   7   79

1. <u>Add.</u>

```
    11        14        15        17        13        12
 + 12      + 14      + 21      + 31      + 14      + 16
 ─────     ─────     ─────     ─────     ─────     ─────
    23
```

```
    22        41        33        82        73        56
 + 12      + 41      + 25      + 14      + 26      + 13
 ─────     ─────     ─────     ─────     ─────     ─────
```

2. <u>Complete</u> each pair of number bonds.

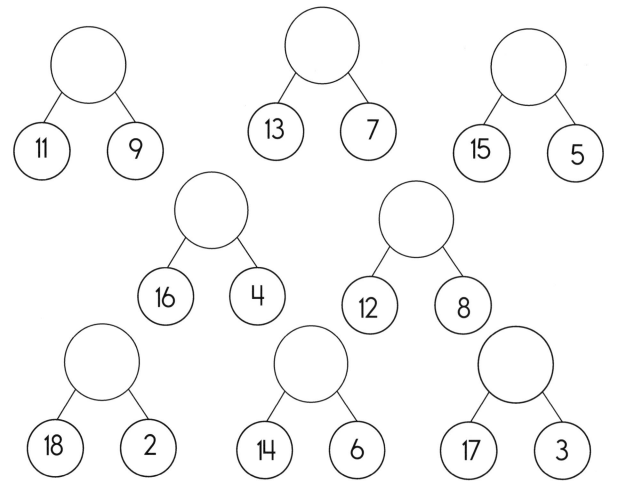

© 2020 Home Run Press, LLC   www.homerunpress.com

1. <u>Subtract.</u>

$$
\begin{array}{r} 25 \\ -\ 3 \\ \hline 22 \end{array}
\qquad
\begin{array}{r} 28 \\ -\ 5 \\ \hline \end{array}
\qquad
\begin{array}{r} 37 \\ -\ 6 \\ \hline \end{array}
\qquad
\begin{array}{r} 33 \\ -\ 2 \\ \hline \end{array}
\qquad
\begin{array}{r} 37 \\ -\ 4 \\ \hline \end{array}
\qquad
\begin{array}{r} 42 \\ -\ 1 \\ \hline \end{array}
$$

$$
\begin{array}{r} 47 \\ -\ 6 \\ \hline \end{array}
\qquad
\begin{array}{r} 56 \\ -\ 5 \\ \hline \end{array}
\qquad
\begin{array}{r} 58 \\ -\ 5 \\ \hline \end{array}
\qquad
\begin{array}{r} 67 \\ -\ 2 \\ \hline \end{array}
\qquad
\begin{array}{r} 69 \\ -\ 4 \\ \hline \end{array}
\qquad
\begin{array}{r} 66 \\ -\ 5 \\ \hline \end{array}
$$

2. <u>Complete</u> each pair of number bonds.

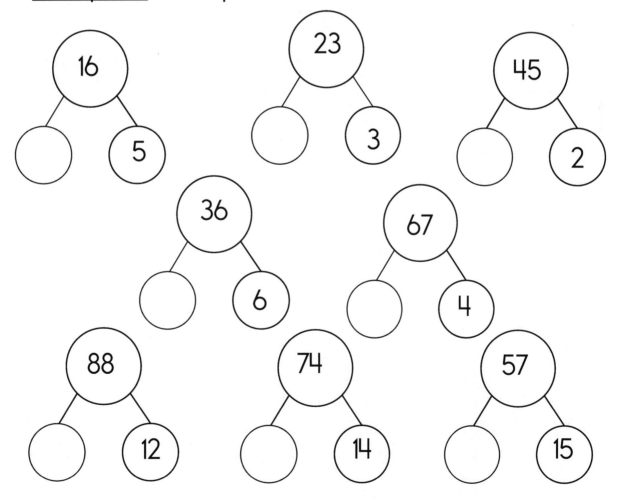

1. <u>Subtract.</u>

34	28	45	37	57	47
- 12	- 14	- 21	- 31	- 14	- 16
22					

22	64	57	39	48	33
- 12	- 41	- 25	- 14	- 26	- 11

2. <u>Complete</u> each pair of number bonds.

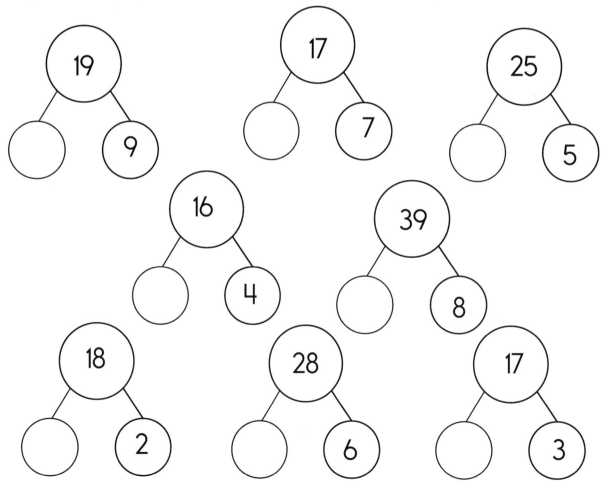

    www.homerunpress.com

1. <u>How many more</u> do I need to add to the second group to make each group the same?

 = 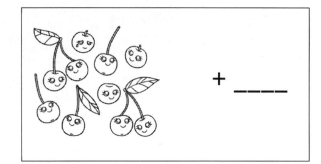 + _____

 =  + _____

 = 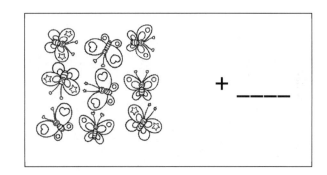 + _____

2. <u>Circle</u> all the combinations that equal 5.

10 – 5   16 – 11   8 – 2

14 – 12   21 – 10   29 – 24

38 – 28   17 – 12   46 - 40

1. If 20 pencils are broken, <u>how many</u> are left?

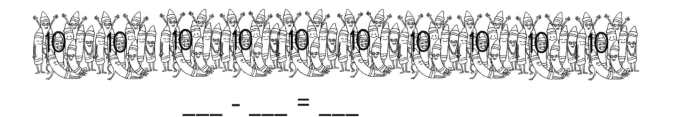

___ - ___ = ___

2. If 30 pencils are broken, <u>how many</u> are left?

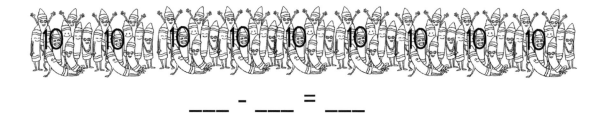

___ - ___ = ___

3. If 50 pencils are broken, <u>how many</u> are left?

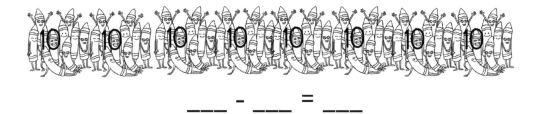

___ - ___ = ___

4. If 40 pencils are broken, <u>how many</u> are left?

___ - ___ = ___

www.homerunpress.com

1. <u>Read</u>. <u>Write</u> how many tens. <u>Write</u> the number.

Three digit numbers are made up of hundreds, tens, and ones.

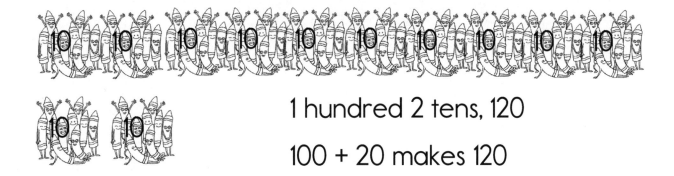

1 hundred 2 tens, 120

100 + 20 makes 120

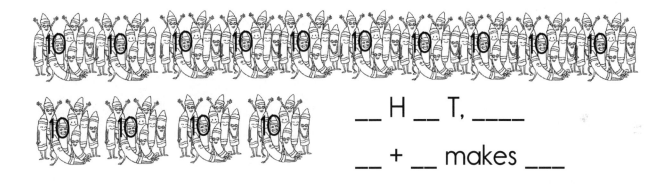

__ H __ T, ____

__ + __ makes ___

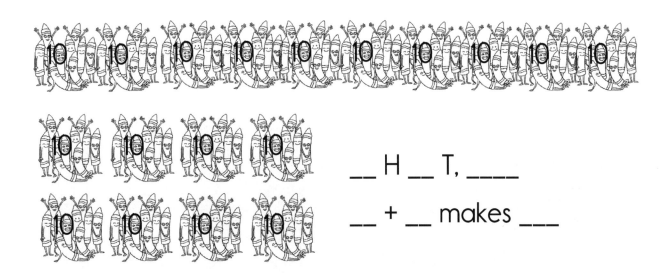

__ H __ T, ____

__ + __ makes ___

1. <u>Add.</u>

100	100	100	100	100	100
+ 25	+ 15	+ 46	+ 12	+ 47	+ 71
125					

120	110	130	120	130	160
+ 6	+ 5	+ 5	+ 2	+ 4	+ 1

2. Complete each pair of number bonds.

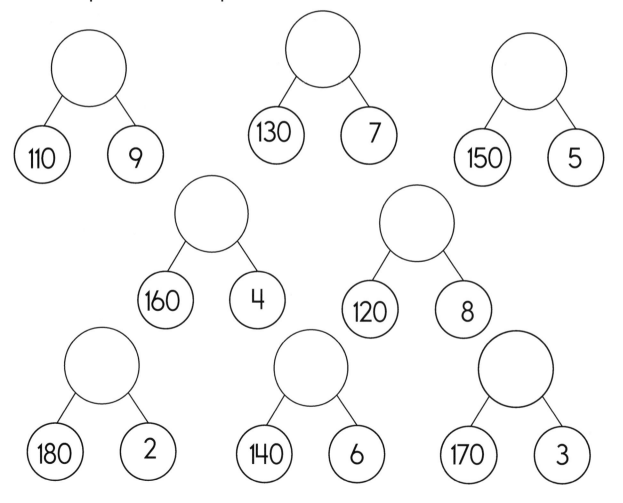

www.homerunpress.com

1. <u>Read.</u>

Place value is the amount a digit is worth in a number.

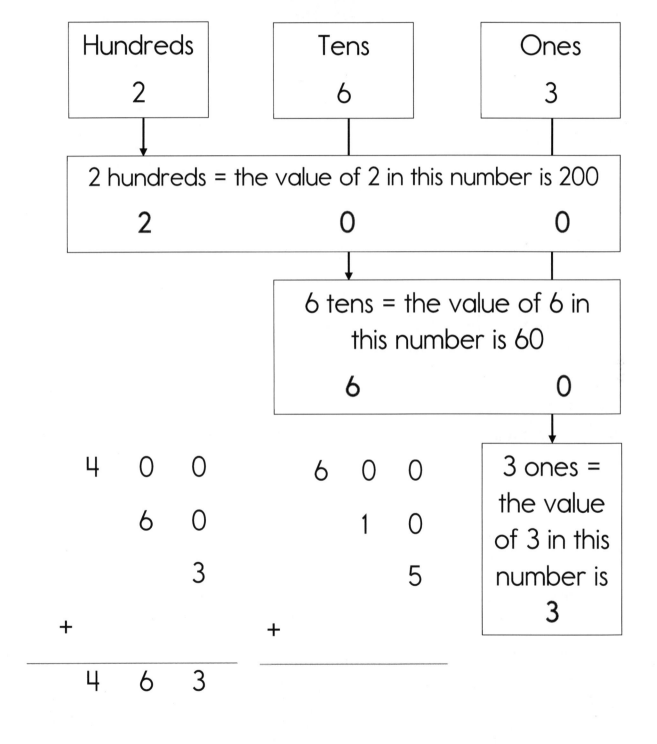

1. <u>What</u> is the value of the 4 in each of these numbers? <u>Circle</u> the right answer.

416	a) Hundreds	b) Tens	c) Ones
914	a) Hundreds	b) Tens	c) Ones
416	a) Hundreds	b) Tens	c) Ones
245	a) Hundreds	b) Tens	c) Ones
624	a) Hundreds	b) Tens	c) Ones

2. <u>Complete</u> each addition number sentence with tens and ones. The first one is done for you.

$45 = 40 + 5$ $61 = \_\_ + \_\_$ $19 = \_\_ + \_\_$

$30 = \_\_ + \_\_$ $74 = \_\_ + \_\_$ $37 = \_\_ + \_\_$

$52 = \_\_ + \_\_$ $65 = \_\_ + \_\_$ $58 = \_\_ + \_\_$

$98 = \_\_ + \_\_$ $87 = \_\_ + \_\_$ $60 = \_\_ + \_\_$

www.homerunpress.com

1. <u>Write</u> the missing numbers.

50 + ___ = 53   ___ + ___ + 7 = 807

20 + ___ = 25   ___ + ___ + 8 = 328

90 + ___ = 96   ___ + ___ + 2 = 972

60 + ___ = 62   ___ + ___ + 0 = 430

10 + ___ = 19   ___ + ___ + 4 = 244

40 + ___ = 48   ___ + ___ + 5 = 595

2. <u>Circle</u> the correct answer.

I have a series of numbers: 0, 2, 4, 6, ___. <u>What</u> is the next number?

a) 10   b) 8   c) 12   d) 7

1. <u>Circle</u> the correct answer.

I have a series of numbers: 1, 2, 4, ___. <u>What</u> is the next number?

   a) 7   b) 8   c) 9   d) 10

2. <u>Color</u> the 2nd frog green. <u>Color</u> the 3rd frog brown. <u>Color</u> the 5th frog black. <u>Color</u> the 6th frog grey.

3. <u>Write</u> the missing numbers.

___ + ___ + ___ = 468   ___ + ___ + ___ = 509

___ + ___ + ___ = 135   ___ + ___ + ___ = 683

___ + ___ + ___ = 245   ___ + ___ + ___ = 248

___ + ___ + ___ = 621   ___ + ___ + ___ = 791

1. <u>Subtract.</u>

146	138	157	134	159	198
- 25	- 15	- 46	- 12	- 47	- 71
121					

127	119	137	126	138	165
- 14	- 15	- 15	- 24	- 31	- 41

2. <u>Complete</u> each pair of number bonds.

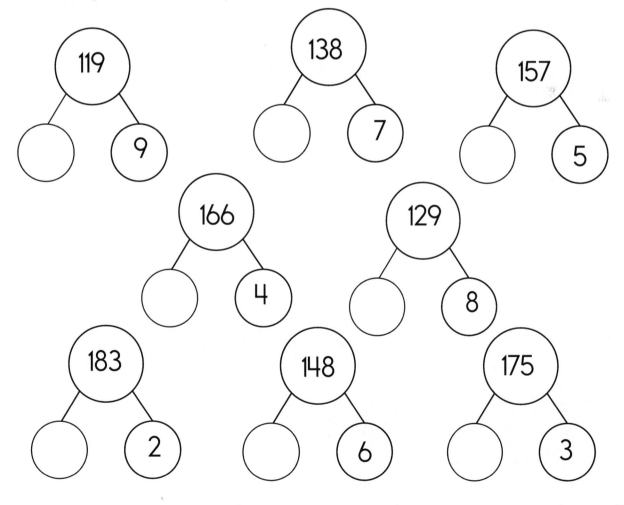

1. Read.

I often need to know if a number is the same as, smaller than, or larger than another <u>number</u>. My teacher calls this comparing numbers. Look at these candies. There are six candies in each row. My teacher says that the number in one row is **equal to** the number in the second row. **6 = 6**

My sister has six candies in the top row and three candies in the bottom row. She says the number in the top row is **greater than** the number in the bottom row. **6 > 3.   6 is greater than 3.**

1. <u>Read</u>.

My brother has five candies in the top row and six candies in the bottom row. He says the number in the top row is **less than** the number in the second row.   5 < 6.   5 is less than 6.

2.   <u>Circle</u> the missing number from the choice box to make the inequality true.

5 < ___ < 9

a) 4   b) 0   c) 6

9 < ___ < 11

a) 7   b) 1   c) 10

15 < ___ < 25

a) 11   b) 20   c) 35

76 < ___ < 90

a) 89   b) 71   c) 100

1. <u>Read.</u>

When I round, I change a number to another number that is almost the same in value, but it is easier to work with.

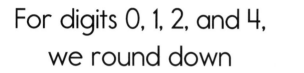

For digits 0, 1, 2, and 4, we round down

For digits 5, 6, 7, 8, and 9, we round up

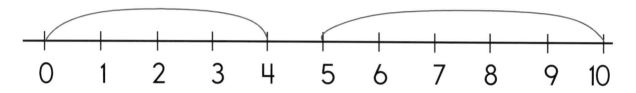

Look at 5<u>2</u>. We look at the ones digit. It's 2.

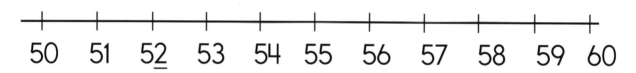

We round down to 50.

Now, look at 5<u>8</u>. The ones digit is 8.

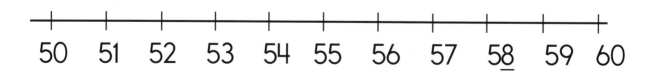

So we round UP to 60.

 www.homerunpress.com

1. <u>Which</u> is more? <u>Compare</u> the numbers using ">," "<," or "=."

3 ones _____ 2 tens   10 ones _____ 1 ten

3 tens _____ 8 ones   2 tens _____ 1 ten

4 tens 2 ones _____ 41 ones

1 ten 2 ones _____ 1 ten 20 ones

2 tens and 3 ones _____ 3 tens and 2 ones

2. <u>Round</u> each number to the nearest 10. <u>Look</u> at the next digit to the right. If it is 0, 1, 2, 3, or 4, then ROUND DOWN, if it is 5, 6, 7, 8, 9, then ROUND UP.

<u>6</u> _____   <u>8</u> _____   <u>5</u> _____

<u>13</u> _____   <u>19</u> _____   <u>16</u> _____

<u>11</u> _____   <u>17</u> _____   <u>19</u> _____

<u>22</u> _____   <u>25</u> _____   <u>23</u> _____

<u>28</u> _____   <u>24</u> _____   <u>29</u> _____

1. <u>Which</u> is more? <u>Write</u> the missing numbers to make the comparison true.

12 ones > ___ ones   7 ones < ___ ten

1 ten = ___ ones   2 tens = ___ ones

5 ones > ___ ones   12 ones < ___ tens

15 ones < ___ ten 6 ones

1 ten 8 ones > 1 ten ___ ones

3 tens and 3 ones = ___ tens and 13 ones

2. <u>Round</u> each number to the nearest 100. <u>Look</u> at the next digit to the right. If it is 0, 1, 2, 3, or 4, then ROUND DOWN, if it is 5, 6, 7, 8, 9, then ROUND UP.

1<u>5</u>3 _____   2<u>0</u>8 _____   7<u>1</u>5 _____

9<u>1</u>3 _____   2<u>5</u>9 _____   2<u>4</u>6 _____

3<u>7</u>1 _____   5<u>5</u>7 _____   4<u>6</u>9 _____

6<u>2</u>2 _____   4<u>8</u>5 _____   9<u>2</u>3 _____

 www.homerunpress.com

1. <u>Read.</u>

Even numbers are made of pairs.

An odd number is always 1 more or 1 less than an even number.

Even numbers end with a digit of 0, 2, 4, 6, 8.

Odd numbers end with a digit of 1, 3, 5, 7, 9.

2. Underline the even numbers.

1, 2, 3, 4, 5, 6, 7, 8, 9, 10, 11, 12, 13, 14, 15, 16

3. Circle the odd numbers.

15, 16, 17, 18, 19, 20, 21, 22, 23, 24, 25, 26

1. Read.

I have tons of candies. I need to estimate because it would take too long to count the exact number. I count 5 candies in the bottom row. There are 4 rows, so I can say there are about 5 + 5 + 5 + 5 candies, which is 20 candies.

column

row

I often don't need to count the candies exactly. If I have two bags of candies that cost the same, I will get the bag with more candies.

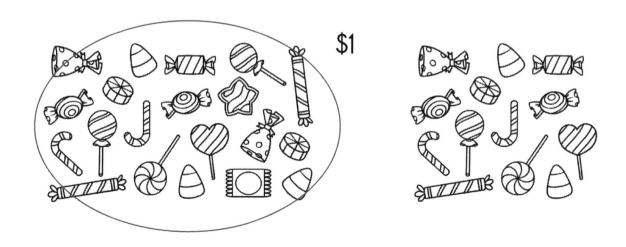

$1

1. I need money to buy objects. <u>Write</u> the missing numbers.

3 coins: 3¢

1 + 1 + __

2 coins: 15¢

10 + __

4 coins: 40¢

3 coins: 3¢

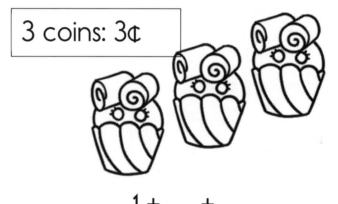

10 + 10 + __ + __

1 + __ + __

2 coins: 10¢

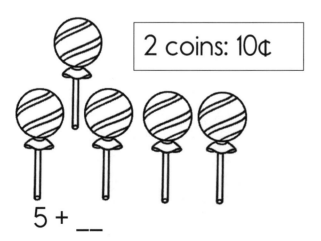

5 + __

I bought 5 lollipops for 10 cents. How much did one lollipop cost?

_____

1. I need money to buy objects. <u>Write</u> the missing numbers.

3 coins: 7¢

5 + 1 + 1

2 coins: 11¢

__ + __

2 coins: 26¢

__ + __

3 coins: 16¢

__ + __ + __

2 coins: 35¢

__ + __

5 coins: 14¢

__ + __ + __ + __ + __

www.homerunpress.com

1. I need money to buy objects. <u>Write</u> the missing numbers.

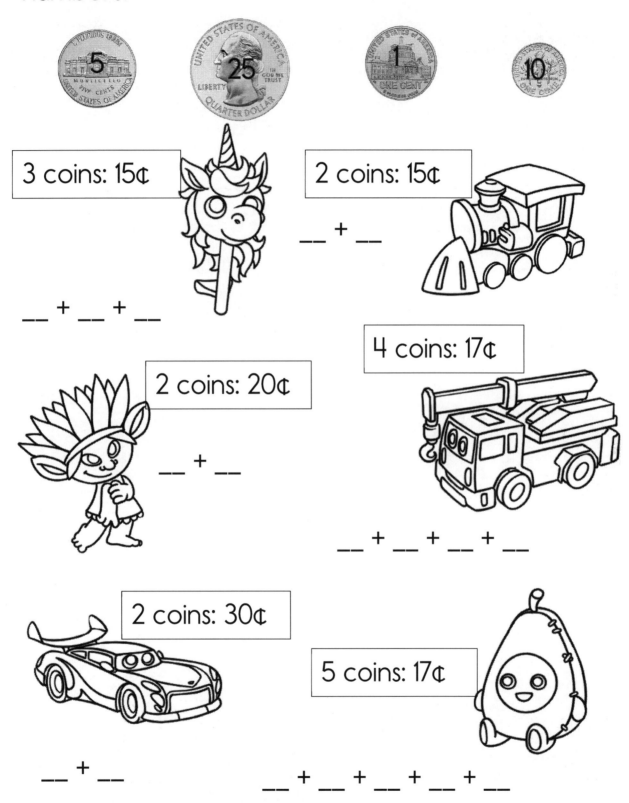

3 coins: 15¢

__ + __ + __

2 coins: 15¢

__ + __

2 coins: 20¢

__ + __

4 coins: 17¢

__ + __ + __ + __

2 coins: 30¢

__ + __

5 coins: 17¢

__ + __ + __ + __ + __

1. <u>Write</u> the missing numbers to make the scales balance.

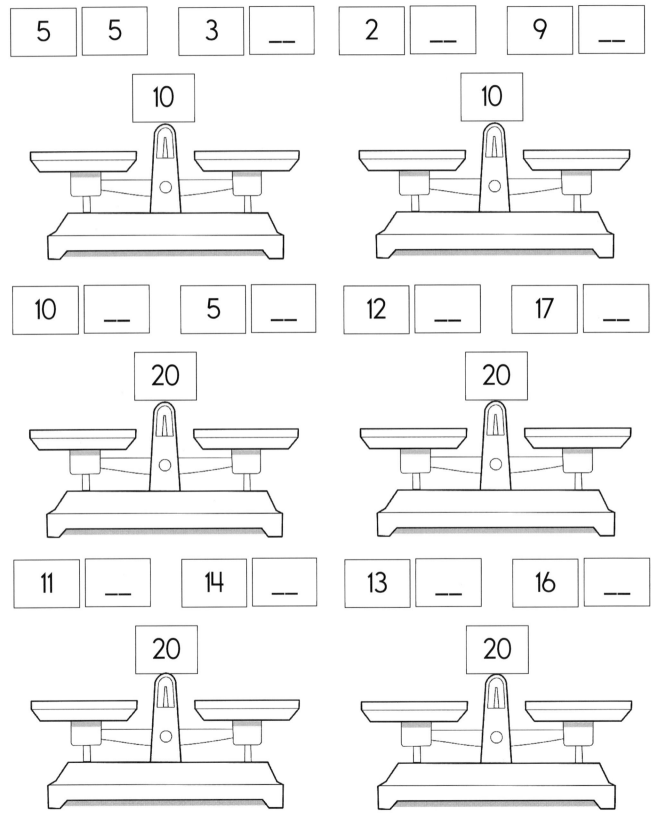

| 5 | 5 | | 3 | __ | | 2 | __ | | 9 | __ |

10   10

| 10 | __ | | 5 | __ | | 12 | __ | | 17 | __ |

20   20

| 11 | __ | | 14 | __ | | 13 | __ | | 16 | __ |

20   20

www.homerunpress.com

1. <u>Write</u> the missing numbers to make the scales balance.

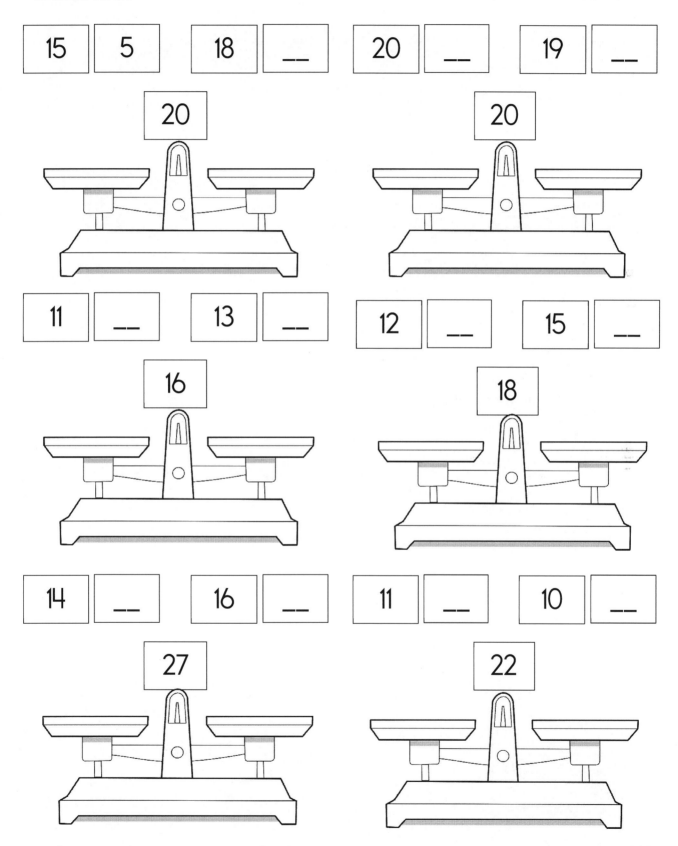

| 15 | 5 | | 18 | __ | | 20 | __ | | 19 | __ |

20

20

| 11 | __ | | 13 | __ | | 12 | __ | | 15 | __ |

16

18

| 14 | __ | | 16 | __ | | 11 | __ | | 10 | __ |

27

22

1. My Grandma baked $\boxed{2}$ pumpkin pies. I ate a $\boxed{\text{half}}$ of the total amount of pies. <u>How many pie(s)</u> are left?

Circle your answer:

0 (1) 2 3 4 5

A half is one of two equal parts of one whole. If two pies are one whole, I could eat 1 pie which is a half. Another half is left. So, I circle 1.

I found $\boxed{4}$ shells. My sister broke a $\boxed{\text{half}}$ of the shells. <u>Color</u> these shells red. <u>How many shells</u> are left?

Circle your answer:

0 1 2 3 4 5

I got $\boxed{6}$ cupcakes. I ate a $\boxed{\text{half}}$ of them. <u>Color</u> the cupcakes I ate. <u>How many cupcakes</u> are left?

Circle your answer:

0 1 2 3 4 5

1. I got 8 candies. I ate a half of the candies. Color them red. How many candies are left?

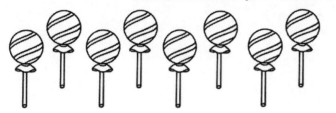

Circle your answer:

0 1 2 3 4 5

I found 10 flowers. A half of the flowers were blooming. How many flowers were not blooming?

Circle your answer:

0 1 2 3 4 5

The pumpkin weighed 2 pounds. We ate a half of it. How many pounds are left?

Circle your answer:

0 1 2 3 4 5

My birthday cake weighed 10 pounds! My friends ate a half of the cake. How many pounds are left?

Circle your answer: 0 1 2 3 4 5

1. <u>What number</u> am I?

Half of me is 1 and double me is 4.

One whole:

A half of two equal parts of one whole is one:

Double means take twice as much or as many:

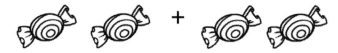

Half of me is 2 and double me is 8.

I am _____.

Half of me is 5 and double me is 20.

I am _____.

Half of me is 10 and double me is 40.

I am _____.

Half of me is 50 and double me is 200.

I am _____.

 www.homerunpress.com

1. When you share equally between two elves, both sets of sweets and fruits have the same amount. <u>Count how many</u> for earch elf?

Each elf must have the same amount.

🍌	🧁	🍊	🍨
____	____	____	____

1. <u>Shade</u> a half for each pair.

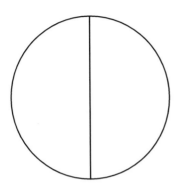 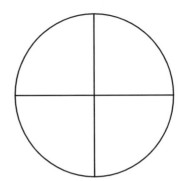

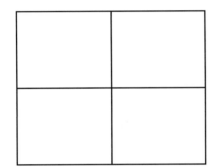 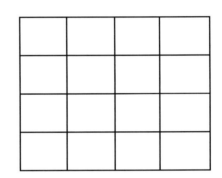

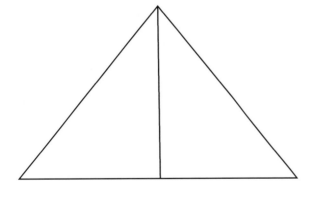 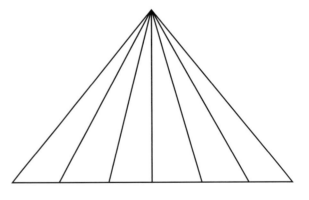

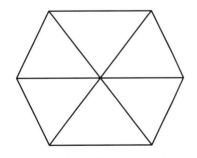 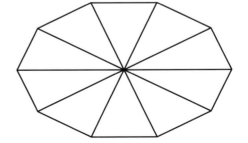

www.homerunpress.com

1. Shade one part out of 8 equal parts.

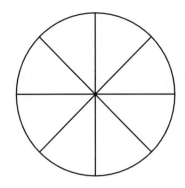 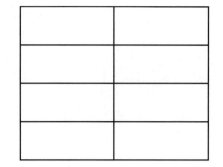

Shade two parts out of 4 equal parts.

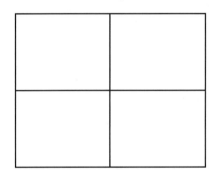 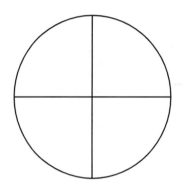

Shade five parts out of 6 equal parts.

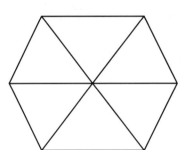 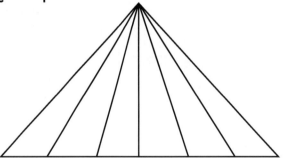

Shade seven parts out of 10 equal parts.

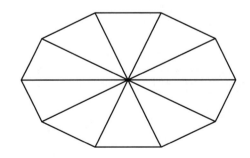 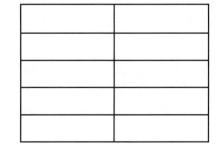

The minute hand is the long hand. It moves 60 minutes. It ponts to the 12 to show the hour's time.

As the minute hand moves around the clock, the hour hand moves from one hour to the next.

The hour hand is the short hand. It points to the hour number.

Read: two thirty

or thirty minutes after two

or thirty minutes before three

Write: 2 : 30

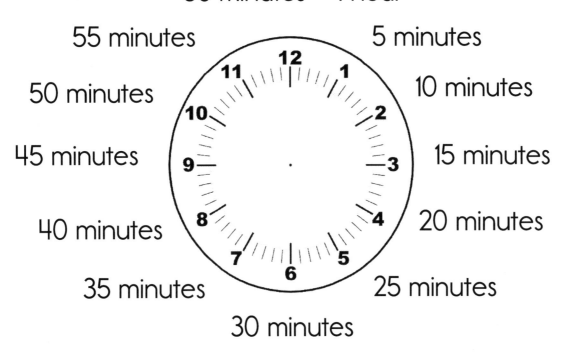

60 minutes = 1 hour

5 minutes

10 minutes

15 minutes

20 minutes

25 minutes

30 minutes

35 minutes

40 minutes

45 minutes

50 minutes

55 minutes

www.homerunpress.com

1. <u>Draw</u> the minute and hour hands to show the time.

1. Draw the minute and hour hands to show the time.

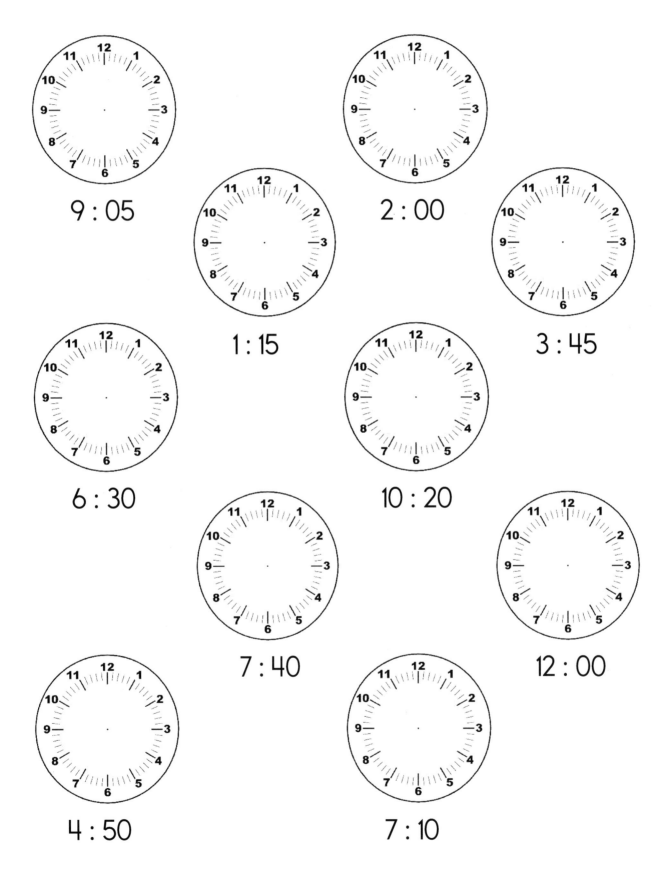

9 : 05

2 : 00

1 : 15

3 : 45

6 : 30

10 : 20

7 : 40

12 : 00

4 : 50

7 : 10

1. I am building a solid slab of rocks: the two rocks next to each other are added to get the number up above. <u>Fill in</u> the missing numbers.

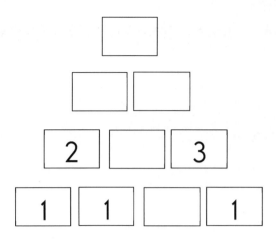

2. <u>Write</u> the numbers in order, from the smallest to the largest.

7, 9, 3, 1, 2, 11, 5, 12, 8, 4, 0, 10, 6

_____

3. Complements to 10. <u>Circle</u> the missing numbers from the choice box to make the equations true.

11 + ___ = 20   a) 8   b) 7   c) 9

5 + ___ = 20   a) 10   b) 5   c) 15

7 + ___ = 20   a) 13   b) 1   c) 14

14 + ___ = 20   a) 4   b) 16   c) 6

1. Circle the right answer.

          a) 25

          b) 30

          c) 35

___ + 25 = 55

2. Complements to 100. Circle the missing numbers from the choice box to make the equations true.

50 + ___ = 100 a) 35 b) 50 c) 60

90 + ___ = 100 a) 10 b) 100 c) 20

20 + ___ = 100 a) 60 b) 20 c) 80

3. Circle the right answer:

I have a series of numbers: 3, 6, 9, 12, __

What is the next number?

 A) 13   B) 15   C) 18   D) 14

4. I have some numbers and signs: 1, 5, 3, +, -.

Write the equation that equals one of the answer choices. _____

 A) 10   B) 7   C) 4   D) 9

   www.homerunpress.com

1. <u>Solve</u> the problem:

1047: the sum of the ones and hundreds is _____.

A) 5
B) 8
C) 7

2. I start at 0 and count on in twos. Will I say 11?

_____

Why? _____

I start at 0 and count on in twos. Will I say 16?

_____

Why? _____

3. <u>Find</u> the value.

853:

The sum of the ones and tens is _____.

The difference between the hundreds and tens is _____.

The difference between the hundreds and ones is _____.

1. <u>Solve</u> the problems:

I had 8 candies. I gave 4 of them to my sister. <u>How many candies</u> has I left?   _____

There are 10 kids at a playground. I counted 7 boys. <u>How many girls</u> are there?

_____

My brother bought 11 chocolate cupcakes and 5 vanilla cupcakes. <u>How many cupcakes</u> did he buy in all?

_____

I found 6 easter eggs. My sister found 4 more Easter eggs than I did. My brother found 7 less Easter eggs than my sister. <u>How many Easter eggs</u> did my brother find?

_____

1. <u>Solve</u> the problems:

I had 15 cupcakes. I ate some cupcakes, and I had 12 cupcakes left. <u>How many cupcakes</u> did I eat?

_____

My brother has 18 trucks and race cars. 3 of them are trucks. <u>How many race cars</u> does he have?

_____

My sister saw 11 butterflies. My brother saw 4 butterflies more than my sister. <u>How many butterflies</u> did they see altogether?

_____

1. <u>Solve</u> the problems:

I had some cupcakes. I ate ⒊ cupcakes and I gave ⒋ cupcakes to my friend. I have ⒒ cupcakes left. <u>How many cupcakes</u> did I have at first?

_____

I had ⒌ yellow balloons and ⒌ more red balloons than yellow balloons. My friend had ⒏ more ballons than I had . <u>How many balloons</u> did my friend have?

_____

There are ⒍ oranges in a basket. My mother puts ⒑ small pears and ⒊ bananas into the basket. <u>How many fruits</u> are there in the basket altogether?

_____

1. Name the shapes shown.

a) square
b) rectangle
c) circle

a) oval
b) square
c) circle

a) circle
b) rectangle
c) diamond

a) triangle
b) square
c) circle

a) triangle
b) rectangle
c) circle

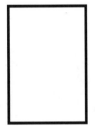

a) circle
b) square
c) rectangle

a) diamond
b) circle
c) triangle

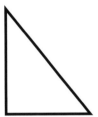

a) circle
b) diamond
c) triangle

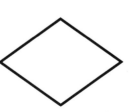

2. Which of the following is **not** a rectangle?

 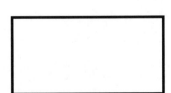 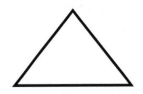 

1. Name the shapes shown.

a) square

b) rectangle

c) circle

a) oval

b) square

c) circle

a) circle

b) rectangle

c) diamond

a) triangle

b) square

c) circle

a) square

b) rectangle

c) circle

a) circle

b) triangle

c) rectangle

a) diamond

b) star

c) triangle

a) heart

b) diamond

c) triangle

2. Which of the following is **not** a triangle?

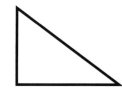 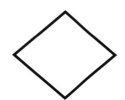 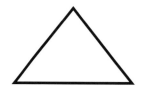 

1. <u>Name</u> each shape. <u>Color</u> the squares yellow, the circles green, the triangles red, and the rectangles blue.

2. <u>Count</u> the number of squares, rectangles, triandles, and circles. <u>Write</u> the word and the number below the shape.

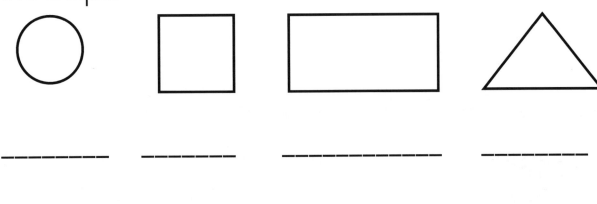

_____   _____   _____   _____

_____   _____   _____   _____

1. The shark is about _____ 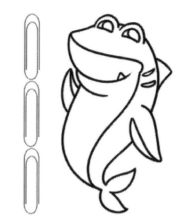 tall.

a) 5

b) 2

c) 3

2. <u>Look</u> at the pictures below.

A   B   C   D   E

The _____ is the tallest toy.

a) cat   b) giraffe

c) monkey   d) penguin

The _____ is the shortest toy.

a) monkey   b) cat

c) cow   d) penguin

          www.homerunpress.com

1. Which elf is the tallest?

a) B

b) A

c) C

A   B   C

2. Which gnome is the shortest?

a) C

b) A

c) B

A   B   C

3. Toy _____ is taller than toy D.

a) B

b) A

c) D

d) C

A   B   C   D

4. Color the shortest toy.

Page 7

1. Read:

Earth is home to billions of animals, birds, plants, and people. People, animals, and plants need clean air to breathe and live. Air is made up of oxygen, nitrogen, carbon dioxide, and other gases. There is water in the air, too. Water makes clouds, rain, snow, and fog. Air around the earth is called the atmosphere.

2. According to the text people and animals need air to

A) breathe   B) live   C) breathe and live

3. Air is made up of

oxygen, nitrogen, carbon dioxide, water, and other gases

4. What word from the text means *you must have it because it is very important?*   need

5. As used in the text, which word could be used instead of *clean?*

A) easy   B) fresh   C) good

Page 8

1. Read:

The Moon looks as big as the Sun. It is made of solid rock, and it is rather close to us. The Sun is shining on the Moon, and it looks like it is **glowing**. Earth is rotating around the Sun while the Moon is rotating around Earth. There are great plains, hills, mountains, and craters on the Moon.

2. What part of speech is the word *moon* as used in the text?

a) Noun   b) Adjective   c) Verb   d) Adverb

3. According to the text the Moon

A) looks huge;
B) looks bigger than Earth;
C) looks smaller than the Sun;
D) looks as big as the Sun.

4. As used in the text, which word could be used instead of *glowing?*

A) dull   B) colorful
C) dark   C) bright

Page 9

1. Read:

Does the Sun rise in the morning? No, it doesn't! The earth turns itself around every twenty-four hours like a spinning ball. At sunrise, the part of the earth is turning towards the Sun. This part has a day. The weather may be cloudy and rainy, but above the clouds, the Sun is always shining. The other part is turning away from the Sun. Their sky is dark, and they have night.

2. Circle TRUE or FALSE to the following statements.

a) TRUE   **FALSE**
The Earth turns around Mars like a spinning ball.

b) TRUE   **FALSE**
When the weather is cloudy and rainy, the Sun is not shining.

c) **TRUE**   FALSE
The Earth turns itself around every 24 hours.

Page 10

1. Read:

A day is the length of time it takes for the earth to spin around its axis. There are 24 hours in a day. A week equals seven days. One month is the length of time it takes for the Moon to rotate around the earth. There are 28, 29, 30, or 31 days in a month. A year is how long it takes for the earth to rotate around the Sun. There are 365 days in a year.

2. According to the text a day

A) is how long it takes to orbit the Moon;
B) is how long it takes to orbit the Sun;
C) is how long it takes to make one full spin of the earth.

3. The Moon rotates around the earth in

A) one day   B) one week   C) one month

4. What word from the text means *being the same in quantity?*   equals

Page 11

1. Read:

Why do we have seasons on the earth? The earth moves around the Sun. It takes a year from start to finish. In December, the northern part of the earth is tilted away from the Sun. This part gets less of the Sun's rays. It has winter. The southern half has summer. In six months, the southern half of the earth is tilted toward the Sun. It has summer. The northern part has winter.

2. The phrase moves around **the Sun** as used in the text refers to:

A) the Sun
B) Mars
C) the earth

3. The word *northern* as used in the text means

A) opposite of summer   B) winter
C) situated on the north   D) summer

4. What word from the text means *the coldest season of the year?*   winter

Page 12

1. Find and circle or cross out the words.

```
F  S  T  X  W  D  R  H  A  E        AFTER
J  N  Y  B  Z  E  M  C  A  N        ALL
G  N  P  A  W  A  R  A  R  O        ABOUT
A  W  M  S  W  O  B  N  T  Y        ACROSS
I  M  N  U  S  L  U  O  N  N        ALMOST
L  A  S  C  E  A  T  U  A           ALWAYS
T  S  O  M  L  A  A  H  X  T        ANOTHER
K  Z  V  N  L  Q  D  E  W  M        ANYONE
A  F  T  E  R  M  D  R  U  M        ASK
L  V  D  N  K  T  A  B  L  W        ANSWER
```

Page 13

1. Read:

People affect the earth in both good and bad ways. All of us make a lot of waste. If the oil spills into the rivers or ocean, this can kill thousands of sea creatures and birds. Villages, cities, and towns throw away a lot of waste into the rivers and lakes. Polluted water can harm people, birds, animals, and plants.

2. Circle the word that does rhyme with the first word in each line.
Words that rhyme end with the same arrangement of letters

house – mouse: right - night

creature
A) feature   B) warfire   C) teacher

throw
A) so   B) know   C) threw

waste
A) based   B) chased   C) taste

Page 14

1. Read:

How can we reduce the bad effects? We can reuse some clothes. We can recycle some materials. The glass waste can be used to make new glass or glass bottles. The waste plastic can be used to make new plastic things. The waste paper can be used to make new paper.

2. Add a question mark to each question.

A question mark (?) is a form of punctuation that comes at the end of a sentence to indicate that a question has been asked.

Words that can be used to ask a question: how, when, what, which, where, why, are, is, was, were.

Why is it important to recycle plastic?

How does the plastic get into the sea?

Do people and animals need clean air?

Where do plants take water?

How can you protect the earth?

Who pollute fresh water?

Page 15

1. Read.

Air contains different gases. People, birds, and animals breathe in oxygen from the air. We need oxygen to live. People breathe out carbon dioxide. Green plants take in carbon dioxide from the air. They return oxygen to the air. This is the way people and plants help each other.

2. As used in the text, which word could be used instead of *contains*?
A) divides B) has
C) adds C) is

3. What do people breathe in?
A) gas B) atmosphere
C) water D) oxygen

4. What do plants breathe in?
A) gas B) carbon dioxide
C) water D) oxygen

5. What word from the text means *to make something easier*? help

Page 16

1. Read.

Are you scared of skeletons? People and some animals have a skeleton in their bodies. The skeleton is the reason why you can stand. Skeletons are made of very hard and strong bones and joints. When we grow and get bigger, a skeleton grows, too. A skeleton protects the body shape and the organs from the inside. We have more than two hundred bones in our skeletons.

2. According to the text,
which statement is correct?
A) skeletons are made up of bones.
B) skeletons are made up of muscles.
C) skeletons are scary.
D) skeletons support our bodies from the inside.

3. When we grow,
A) a skeleton changes B) we get smaller
C) a skeleton moves C) a skeleton grows

Page 17

1. Read.

What makes my heart beat? When I sit still and watch cartoons, my heart beats slower. When I am running a race with my friend, my heart beats faster. My teacher says it happens because my body needs more oxygen. My brain makes my heart beat automatically. It never stops beating, even when I am asleep. When my heart beats or pumps, it pushes blood to every part of my body and back again.

2. Write the numbers 1 to 4 to show the correct order in which events occurred in the
4 It never stops beating.
2 My heart beats slower.
1 What makes my heart beat?
3 My brain makes my heart beat automatically.

3. Which statement is correct?
A) The blood delivers oxygen to every part of my body.
B) I have to remember to make my heart beat.

Page 18

1. Read.

Ears help me hear. I hear my mom calling me to dinner. I hear my brother honking for me to get out of the way. Sounds reach my ears, and messages are sent to the brain. The brain tells me what the sound means. It happens very fast.

2. Circle one of the four words that means almost the same as the first word.
Synonyms are words that have similar meanings:

tell A) open B) say C) move D) yell
call A) shout B) whisper C) do D) slow
fast A) quiet B) quick C) aloud D) slow
reach A) leave B) start C) get D) fail

3. Circle one of the four words that means the opposite of the first word.
Antonyms are words that have opposite meanings:

send A) post B) receive C) mail D) make
slow A) good B) huge C) fast D) easy
get A) give B) win C) buy D) grab

Page 19

1. Read.

There is one long backbone inside a snake's body. It is made up of many small bones. A snake moves by making its skin crawl. When a snake moves, the muscles bend, and the edges of the scales grip the ground. That is why a snake moves faster on a rough surface. It cannot push its body on smooth ground. It moves in curves.

2. According to the text, which statement is correct?
A) A snake's body is long.
B) A snake's body is smooth.
C) A snake's body is made of many long backbones.
D) A snake's backbone is made of many small bones.

3. A snake moves
A) in a straight line B) on Monday
C) in curves

Page 20

1. Read.

Glass is transparent. That means you can see through it. Glass is clear, and it lets the light shine through. We use glass for windows. It lets sunlight into the room. Eyeglasses use special lenses to help a person with eye problems see better. Some eyeglasses help people see far things clearly. Other glasses help people see near things clearly.

2. As used in the text, which word could be used instead of *transparent*?
A) fresh B) clear
C) white C) open

3. What do people use glass for?
A) walls B) windows
C) toys D) trees

4. According to the text eyeglasses help people
A) tell the time B) see things clearly
C) see things at night D) make shadows

Page 21

1. Read.

When autumn comes, the leaves change color. They turn yellow, gold, red, orange, and brown. It's getting colder. Trees find it difficult to get water from the ground. So the leaves dry out and drop to the ground. The twigs and branches are bare. Some trees do not lose their leaves. Pine trees have thick needles that help keep the trees from losing water. That means they are evergreens because their leaves, or needles, are always green.

2. The purpose of this text is to
A) inform B) persuade C) entertain

3. Circle the words that could describe the color of the leaves in the fall.
black yellow purple red orange brown

4. Why do some trees stay green?
A) they have strong leaves B) they are very old
C) the leaves are thick D) their needles are thick

Page 22

1. Read.

Who makes a rainbow? Sunlight is made up of lots of different colors. When it's raining, the sun shines through the tiny raindrops in the air. The water makes the sunlight spread into different colors. The colors appear in the same order: red, orange, yellow, green, blue, indigo, and violet. On a sunny day, you can make a rainbow! Turn on the sprinkler and see a rainbow in the spray!

2. Which word could be used instead of *appear* as it is used in the text?
A) are seen B) show C) end

3. The word *sunny* has a similar meaning to
A) rainy B) bright C) dull

4. The text provides
A) facts B) warnings
C) explanations D) amusements

5. What word from the text means *to create*? make

131

Page 26

1. Find and circle or cross out the words.

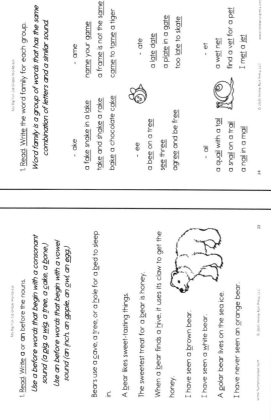

Word search grid

WRITE	WAY	WATER	YELLOW
AIR	AROUND	ANOTHER	ALSO
ASKED	BACK	BEFORE	BOOK
BECAUSE	EARTH	GROUP	GIRL
DIFFERENT	GOOD	EVEN	EXAMPLE

Page 30

1. Underline five adjectives for each picture.

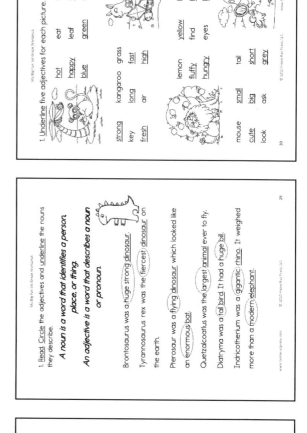

strong	hot	eat	banana
key	happy	leaf	tail
fresh	blue	green	cloud

kangaroo	grass	yellow	lion
long	fast	find	huge
air	high	eyes	large

mouse	small	tail
cute	big	short
look	ask	grey

Page 25

1. Read Find and write the missing word that makes the best sense in each sentence. Capitalize the first word of a sentence.

there were _____ than 2000 gods in Ancient Egypt.

a) more b. as c. much

the Egyptians started to _____ pyramids more than four thousands years ago.

a. need b) build c. move

it took _____ of workers and more than 2 million blocks to make the Great Pyramid.

a. tens b. ones c.) thousands

the largest statue in the _____ world was the Sphinx.

a. modern b) ancient c. far

it had the _____ of a lion and the head of a man.

a) body b. leg c. ears

Page 29

1. Read. Circle the adjectives and underline the nouns they describe.

A noun is a word that identifies a person, place, or thing.

An adjective is a word that describes a noun or pronoun.

Brontosaurus was a huge strong dinosaur.

Tyrannosaurus rex was the fiercest dinosaur on the earth.

Pterosaur was a flying dinosaur which looked like an enormous bat.

Quetzalcoatlus was the largest animal ever to fly.

Diatryma was a tall bird. It had a huge bill.

Indricotherium was a gigantic rhino. It weighed more than a modern elephant.

Page 24

1. Read. Write the word family for each group.

Word family is a group of words that has the same combination of letters and a similar sound

- ake

a fake snake in a lake
take and shake a rake
bake a chocolate cake

- ame

name your game
a frame is not the same
came to tame a tiger

- ee

a bee on a tree
see three
agree and be free

- ate

a late date
a plate in a gate
too late to skate

- ail

a quail with a tail
a snail on a trail
a nail in a mail

- et

a wet net
find a vet for a pet
I met a jet

Page 28

1. Underline four nouns for each picture.

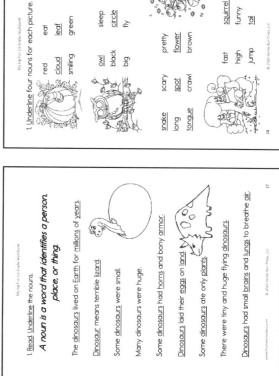

red	eat	worm
cloud	leaf	sweet
smiling	green	watermelon

owl	sleep	tree
black	circle	round
big	fly	twig

pretty
flower
brown

snake	fast	squirrel	tall
long	high	funny	autumn
tongue	jump	tail	grass
scary	spot	crawl	

Page 23

1. Read. Write a or an before the nouns.

Use a before words that begin with a consonant sound (a pig, a wig, a tree, a cake, a bone.)

Use an before words that begin with a vowel sound (an inch, an apple, an owl, an egg.)

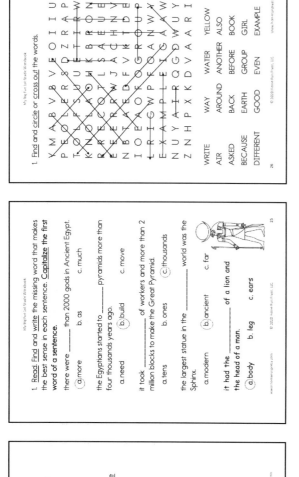

Bears use a cave, a tree, or a hole for a bed to sleep in.

A bear likes sweet-tasting things.

The sweetest treat for a bear is honey.

When a bear finds a hive, it uses its claw to get the honey.

I have seen a brown bear.

I have seen a white bear.

A polar bear lives on the sea ice.

I have never seen an orange bear.

Page 27

1. Read. Underline the nouns.

A noun is a word that identifies a person, place, or thing.

The dinosaur lived on Earth for millions of years.

Dinosaur means terrible lizard.

Some dinosaurs were small.

Many dinosaurs were huge.

Some dinosaurs had horns and bony armor.

Dinosaurs laid their eggs on land.

Some dinosaurs ate only plants.

There were tiny and huge flying dinosaurs.

Dinosaurs had small brains and lungs to breathe air.

1. Read **Use** the the words ("try", "tried", "turns", "turn", or "turned") to write the correct verb tense for each sentence. **Capitalize the pronoun I**

Verb tenses (past, present, future) tell if the action takes place in the past (I liked chocolate ice-cream), present (I like vanilla ice-cream), or future (I will see you tomorrow).

I usually try hard not to laugh when I watch "Trolls."

I tried hard not to laugh when I was watching "Trolls."

I will try harder to read more.

The weather usually turns colder in November.

In the fall, leaves turned color.

My brother will turn ten next year.

34

---

1. Read **Draw** a line from the contraction to the two words for which it stands.

don't — you are
he'll — would not
I'm — does not
can't — he is
we're — will not
hasn't — I am
aren't — I have
you're — you have
you've — he will
couldn't — can not
isn't — is not
I've — do not
doesn't — we are
he's — are not
won't — has not
I'll — could not
wouldn't

38

---

1. Read **Circle** the verb in each sentence. *Verbs are words that show action.*

A dog is a furry animal with four legs.

A young dog is called a puppy.

There are many kinds of dogs.

Dogs make good pets.

A dog uses its tail when it wants to talk to people or to other dogs.

When a puppy wags its tail, it may want to play.

When a puppy puts its tail between its legs, it is scared.

When dogs want to play, they bark.

Some dogs bark when they get angry.

Other dogs bark when they want to tell their owner about a stranger near the house.

33

---

1. Read **Change** two words in each sentence to a contraction and **rewrite** the sentence. **Use** the contractions from the Choice Box.

Contractions are shortened words, where you use an apostrophe (') in place of the missing letters.

| can't | doesn't | you're | it's |

When it is very cold, clouds are cold, too.

When it's very cold, clouds are cold, too.

The Sun does not go anywhere at night.

The Sun doesn't go anywhere at night.

You cannot feel the earth moving because you are moving with it.

You can't feel the earth moving because you're moving with it.

37

---

1. Find and **circle** or **cross out** the words.

(word search grid)

HELP   HOME   HOUSE   INSIDE
KNOW   KIND   LEAVE   LIVE
LINE   LARGE LAND   LETTERS
LEARN MOST   MUCH   MEANS
MAN   MOVE   MOTHER NIGHT

32

---

1. Read **Circle** and **write** in the missing word. *Homophones are words that are spelled differently but sound the same.*

A bear (bear/bare)'s color helps it to find food when the trees are bare (bear/bare).

A bored (board/bored) bear likes to catch fish.

Sometimes a bear sits on a board (board/bored) and waits for fish to swim by.

A bee (be/bee) makes its honey from flowers.

So the hive and honey can be (be/bee) sweet for the bears.

A spider makes webs to trap insects for (for/four) food.

Four (For/four) flies were caught in the trap.

36

---

1. Read **Circle** the right adjective to describe the noun.

animal
a. walk   b. do   c. white   d. purple

bird
a. bee   b. thick   c. tiny   d. easy

land
a. close   b. green   c. begin   d. plant

sea
a. blue   b. year   c. net   d. early

dinosaur
a. new   b. huge   c. about   d. south

rock
a. rainy   b. warm   c. solid   d. open

whale
a. fly   b. hot   c. wood   d. long

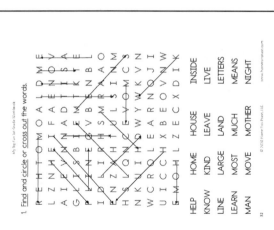

31

---

1. Read and **write** the correct tense of the verb. **Use** the words **present, past, or future.**

Sharks are heavy.   present

If sharks stop swimming, they will sink.   future

The shark looked hungry.   past

Dolphins are small whales.   present

The dolphine made whistles and clicks.   past

Most of dolphins will live in the ocean.   future

Whales live in the ocean, too.   present

The blue whale is the largest animal.   present

Ichthyosaurs were as big as blue whales.   past

When whales want to play, they will dive under a bunch of seaweed.   future

Present   future

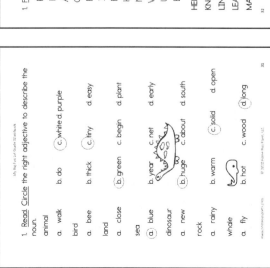

35

133

Page 39

1. Find and circle or cross out the words.

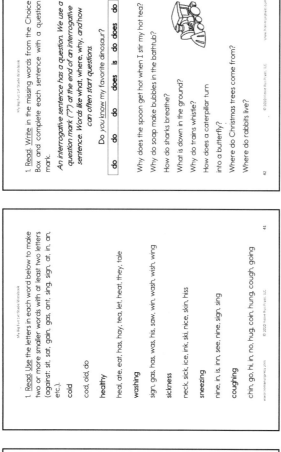

RIVER	RUN	QUESTION	REALLY
SCHOOL	STARTED	SAW	STORY
SEA	STATE	SOMETHING	SEEMED
SONG	SECOND	THOUGHT	TOOK
WATCH	WALKED	TOGETHER	THOSE

Page 40

1. Use each fragment to create and write a complete sentence. Read each sentence.

A complete sentence is a group of words that form a complete thought.

I am kind and helpful.

A sentence fragment is a group of words that do not form a complete thought.

I am kind. And helpful.

I catch a cold. From germs.

I catch a cold from germs.

These germs. Are called viruses.

These germs are called viruses.

Viruses are tiny complicated molecules. That float in the air.

Viruses are tiny complicated molecules that float in the air.

Page 41

1. Read. Use the letters in each word below to make two or more smaller words with at least two letters (against: sit, sat, gain, gas, ant, sing, sign, at, in, an, etc.).

cold — cod, old, do

healthy — heal, ate, eat, has, hay, tea, let, heat, they, tale

washing — sign, gas, has, was, his, saw, win, wash, wish, wing

sickness — neck, sick, ice, ink, ski, nice, skin, hiss

sneezing — nine, in, is, inn, see, nine, sign, sing

coughing — chin, go, hi, in, no, hug, coin, hung, cough, going

Page 42

1. Read. Write in the missing words from the Choice Box and complete each sentence with a question mark.

An interrogative sentence has a question. We use a question mark ("?") at the end of an interrogative sentence. Words like what, where, why, and how can often start questions.

Do you know my favorite dinosaur?

do	do	does	is	do	does	do

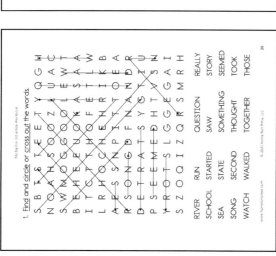

Why does the spoon get hot when I stir my hot tea?

Why do soap make bubbles in the bathtub?

How do sharks breathe?

What is down in the ground?

Why do trains whistle?

How does a caterpillar turn into a butterfly?

Where do Christmas trees come from?

Where do rabbits live?

Page 43

1. Read the words. Write the word that is a whole thing and then, the words that are parts of the whole.

baby	boy	kids	girl
Whole	kids		
Parts	baby	boy	girl

books	library	librarian	magazines
Whole	library		
Parts	books	librarian	magazines

student	teacher	classroom	school
Whole	school		
Parts	student	teacher	classroom

read	write	teacher	classroom
Whole	learn		
Parts	read	write	add	learn

left	forward	add	right
Whole	direction		
Parts	left	right	forward

Page 44

1. Rewrite the words in order from highest to lowest in size or degree.

nice, great, bad — great, nice, bad

better, good, best — best, better, good

2. Unscramble a compound word.

A compound word is formed when two words are joined together to make a new word.

ridb + eohus — birdhouse — a box to provide for a bird

ni + tesd — inside — the inner part of something

ands + obx — sandbox — kids play with sand in it

otne + koob — notebook — you write notes in it

Page 45

1. Look at the words and think about how they are related. Find the missing word in the list and write it.

back is to front as closed is to _____ open

a. open   b. add   c. stop

(a. open — circled)

runner is to runs as worker is to works

a. plays   (b. works — circled)   c. talks

2. Use the code to find out the word.

w=ß r=Ö a=£ y=Â h=Ø o=∞

ßØÂ — why   ßÖωte — wrote

ßØ£t — what   Ø£Öd — hard

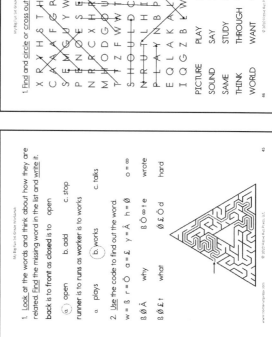

Page 46

1. Find and circle or cross out the words.

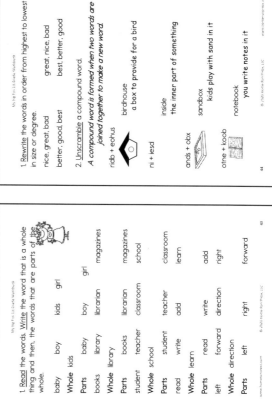

PICTURE	PLAY	POINT	PAGE
SOUND	SAY	SHOW	SET
SAME	STUDY	SHOULD	SPELL
THINK	THROUGH	THREE	TURN
WORLD	WANT	WHY	VERY

1. Read Write the best synonym from the choice box.
Synonyms are words that have the same or almost the same meaning.

guys	stone	go	learn	watch
far	Mom	mad	pay	washed
say	make	big	gate	nap	happy

move	go	talk	say
sleep	nap	clean	washed
glad	happy	large	big
spend	pay	door	gate
miles	far	men	guys
angry	mad	build	make
study	learn	rock	stone
mother	Mom	look	watch

---

1. Read Circle the best synonym in the list.
Synonyms are words that have the same or almost the same meanings.

close	a) near	b. hand	c. open
right	a. left	b) correct	c. false
paint	a) color	b. write	c. erase
cry	a. sing	b. bring	c) weep
sad	a. glad	b) unhappy	c. joy
foot	a. body	b) leg	c. run
car	a. plane	b) vehicle	c. train
glove	a) mitten	b. hat	c. shoe
children	a. boys	b. girls	c) kids
wide	a. short	b) large	c. cut
fine	a. bad	b. kind	c) great
tame	a) pet	b. strong	c. wild

---

1. Read Write the best antonym from the choice box.
Antonyms are words that have the opposite meanings.

night	full	glad	dirty	big	come
short	take	noise	future	near
found	light	bottom	cold	asleep

silence	noise	day	night
awake	asleep	sad	glad
past	future	far	near
top	bottom	clean	dirty
lost	found	hot	cold
long	short	empty	full
little	big	heavy	light
go	come	give	take

---

1. Read Circle the best antonym in the list.
Antonyms are words that have the opposite meanings.

beginning	a. start	b. opening	c) end
kind	a. cool	b. nice	c) mean
close	a. do	b) open	c. walk
seek	a. explore	b) hide	c. play
best	a. good	b. bad	c) worst
quiet	a) noisy	b. whisper	c. wild
beautiful	a. red	b) ugly	c. wonderful
big	a. huge	b. large	c) tiny
longer	a. taller	b) shorter	c. higher
catch	a) throw	b. play	c. ball
black	a. red	b) white	c. sky

---

1. Read Circle the best antonym in the list.
Antonyms are words that have the opposite meanings.

sometimes	a. now	b. there	c) often
heavy	a. thin	b. big	c) light
cry	a. shout	b) laugh	c. sing
soon	a. shortly	b. late	c) now
agree	a. confirm	b) disagree	c. reply

2. Use the code to find out the word.

r = ß   e = Õ   l = £   g = Â   a = Ø   n = ∞

s ∞ o w	snow	h Ø p p y	happy
∞ i c Õ	nice	£ i ∞ Õ	line
s m Ø l l	small	c ß Õ Õ p	creep
£ Ø ß Â Õ	large	c ß Ø w £	crawl

---

1. Unscramble the words.

| sith | terwa | cplae |
| fish | water | place |

2. Read Circle the 15 errors in the story. Write the corrections above each error.

Once upon a time a small fish lived in a wonderful place. It loved the warm waters in spring and the beautiful coral. Every morning it was happy to open its eyes and say, "Good morning"

It used its fins like paddles to push through the water. It got the oxygen from water. It breathed through special body parts called gills. It travelled in a group of fish called a school. They travelled like that for protection if a big fish attacked.

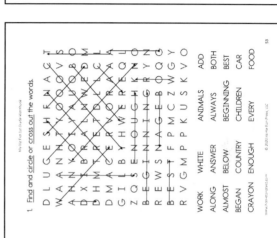

---

1. Find and circle or cross out the words.

```
D L U G E S H R N A C T
W A A N H T X O Q O V S
A X N X O T Y A U O B O
D X T B R A L N V E D M
B H M T R E T D L G L A
D M A C E R V O R A X L
G I L B Y H W E R E Q L
Z Q S E N O U G H K N O
B E G I N N I N G R Y N
R E W S N A G E B O Q G
B E S T F P M C Z W G Y
R V G M P P K U S K V O
```

WORK	WHITE	ANIMALS	ADD
ALONG	ANSWER	ALWAYS	BOTH
ALMOST	BELOW	BEGINNING	BEST
BEGAN	COUNTRY	CHILDREN	CAR
CRAYON	ENOUGH	EVERY	FOOD

---

1. Look at the words and think about how they are related. Find the missing word in the list and write it.

| stand | point | page | first |

carpet is to rug as dot is to _____ point
word is to letter as book is to _____ page
out is to in as sit is to _____ stand
light is to heavy as last is to _____ first

2. Look at the words and think about how they are related. Circle the right letter.

whistle | return | wear
a) adjective   b) noun   c) verb

circle | square | triangle
a) direction   b) shape   c) change

cm | ruler | inch
a) add   b) geometry   c) counting

Page 55

1. **Read** Find and <u>write</u> the missing word that makes the best sense in each sentence.

Romans lived in Rome more than 2000 years ago.
   a. stood   b. moved   (c.) lived

The best Roman houses had glass windows.
   a. toys   (b.) houses   c. cars

Most kids did not go to school.
   (a.) school   b. library   c. party

Children learned to write, read, and basic math.
   a. play   (b.) read   c. clean

Romans discovered how to make concrete.
   a. glue   b. stick   (c.) make

Romans built straight roads, bridges, and tunnels where possible.
   a. bricks   (b.) bridges   c. stores

Page 56

1. <u>Look</u> at the words and think about how they are related. <u>Find</u> the missing word in the list and <u>write</u> it.

yellow, black, brown, _____
   a. kind   b. stop   (c.) white

mammals, birds, reptiles, insects: _____
   a. things   (b.) animals   c. humans

task, problem, question: _____
   (a.) learn   b. play   c. sing

job, duty, effort, _____
   (a.) work   b. relax   c. talk

bedroom, living room, kitchen, _____
   a. home   b. company   (c.) study

paper   book   _____   library
   (a.) school   b. store   c. playground

Page 57

1. **Read** Write the missing word ('far,' 'farther,' or 'further').

The word further refers to time or amount.

The legend about Sparta goes further back to the ancient times. Sparta had two kings. Most people were slaves. Spartans did not work at all. They dedicated themselves to becoming the greatest warriors in the world. The boys left their families at the age of 7. Girls were educated and competed in sports, too. Further information about Spartans is available in books about ancient Greece.

The words far and farther refer to length or distance.

What distance did the kids jump? The boy jumped far.

The girl jumped farther.

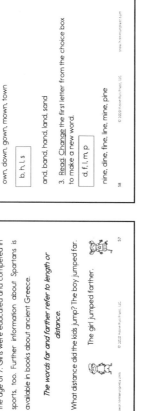

Page 58

1. **Read** <u>Use</u> the letters in each word below to make two or more smaller words with at least two letters (against: sit, sat, again.)

notice   not, ice, tie, ant, nice, once, note, on, ten

often   ten, to, no, on, not, net, of, one, ton, toe

2. **Read** <u>Add</u> one letter from the choice box to make a new word.

| d, g, m, t |
own, down, gown, mown, town

| b, h, l, s |
and, band, hand, land, sand

3. **Read** <u>Change</u> the first letter from the choice box to make a new word.

| d, f, l, m, p |
nine, dine, fine, mine, pine

Page 59

1. <u>Look</u> at the words and think about how they are related or alike. <u>Circle</u> the right letter.

object   thing   item
   (A.) piece   B. answer   C. book

pond   lake   sea
   A. island   (B.) ocean   C. earth

flowers   trees   bushes
   A. alive   B. blooming   (C.) plants

leaves   twigs   branches
   (A.) trees   B. spring   C. grow

2. <u>Look</u> at the words and think about how they are related. <u>Continue</u> a sequence using a word from the list.

story   tomorrow   [something]

nothing, anything, _____ → something

yesterday, today, _____ → tomorrow

letters, words, sentences, _____ → story

Page 60

1. <u>Find</u> and circle or cross out the words.

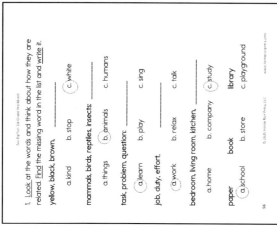

FEET	FACE	FAMILY	GROW
HARD	HIGH	IMPORTANT	ICE
KNOW	KEEP	LIGHT	LAST
LIFE	LIST	LATER	MIGHT
NEVER	NIGHT	OFTEN	OBJECT

Page 61

1. **Read**

When I add 3 candies and 2 candies, there are 5 candies altogether. It does not matter which way I add candies together.

3 + 2 = 5 candies

+   means add or plus

means equals → 2 + 3 = 5 candies

I add 4 cars and 3 trucks.

I have 4 cars and 3 trucks together. I can find the total simply by counting them all. There are 7 in all.

4 + 3 = 7

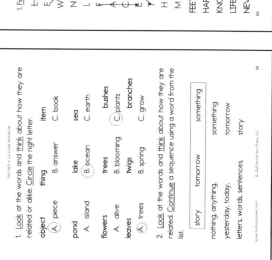

Page 62

1. **Read**

I use a number line to find out the answer when I add 4 and 2. First, I <u>draw</u> a line and <u>mark</u> it with numbers. I find 4 on the number line.

Start counting at 4.

0 1 2 3 4 5 6 7 8 9 10

I need to add 2, so I jump 2 places to the right.

0 1 2 3 4 5 6 7 8 9 10

This takes me to 6.

4 + 2 = 6

So

I add 30 and 50. First, I find 30. Then, I jump 5 places to the right.

0 10 20 30 40 50 60 70 80 90 100

30 + 50 = 80

So

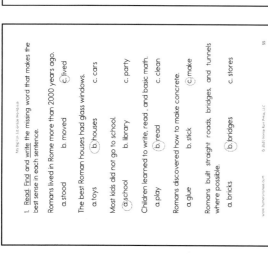

(page 66)

My Big Fun 1st Grade Workbook

1. Add

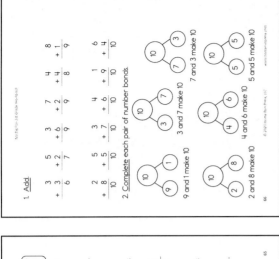

$$\begin{array}{r}3\\+3\\\hline6\end{array}\qquad\begin{array}{r}5\\+2\\\hline7\end{array}\qquad\begin{array}{r}3\\+6\\\hline\end{array}\qquad\begin{array}{r}7\\+2\\\hline\end{array}\qquad\begin{array}{r}4\\+4\\\hline8\end{array}$$

$$\begin{array}{r}2\\+8\\\hline\end{array}\qquad\begin{array}{r}3\\+5\\\hline\end{array}\qquad\begin{array}{r}3\\+7\\\hline\end{array}\qquad\begin{array}{r}1\\+9\\\hline\end{array}\qquad\begin{array}{r}6\\+4\\\hline10\end{array}$$

2. Complete each pair of number bonds.

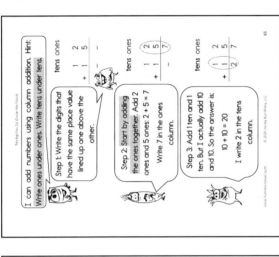

9 and 1 make 10

3 and 7 make 10

2 and 8 make 10

4 and 6 make 10

7 and 3 make 10

5 and 5 make 10

(page 70)

My Big Fun 1st Grade Workbook

1. Read

I use a number line to find out the answer when I subtract 4 from 7. First, I draw a line and mark with numbers. I find 7 on the number line.

Start counting at 7.

0 1 2 3 4 5 6 7 8 9 10

I need to take away 4, so I jump 4 places to the left.

This takes me to 3.

So $7 - 4 = 3$

0 1 2 3 4 5 6 7 8 9 10

I subtract 40 from 60. First, I find 60. Then, I jump 4 places to the left.

0 10 20 30 40 50 60 70 80 90 100

So $60 - 40 = 20$

(page 65)

My Big Fun 1st Grade Workbook

I can add numbers using **column addition**. Hint: Write ones under ones. Write tens under tens.

Step 1: Write the digits that have the same place value lined up one above the other.

$$\begin{array}{cc}\text{tens} & \text{ones}\\1 & 2\\+\;1 & 5\\\hline\end{array}$$

Step 2: Start by adding the ones together. Add 2 ones and 5 ones: $2 + 5 = 7$. Write 7 in the ones column.

$$\begin{array}{cc}\text{tens} & \text{ones}\\1 & 2\\+\;1 & 5\\\hline & 7\end{array}$$

Step 3: Add 1 ten and 1 ten. But I actually add 10 and 10. So the answer is:
$10 + 10 = 20$
I write 2 in the tens column.

$$\begin{array}{cc}\text{tens} & \text{ones}\\1 & 2\\+\;1 & 5\\\hline 2 & 7\end{array}$$

(page 69)

My Big Fun 1st Grade Workbook

Subtraction is the opposite of addition. Subtraction means finding the difference between two numbers or taking away from a number. When I give 2 candies to my sister out of 3 candies that I have, how many candies are left?

means equals   means subtract or minus

3 - 2 = 1 candy

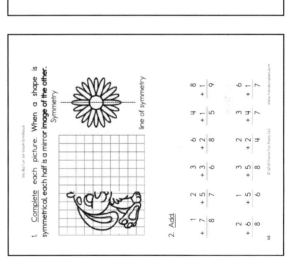

When I subtract or take away 2 cars from the 4 cars that my brother has, he is left with 2 cars.

4 - 2 = 2

He has 4 cars and I take away 2 cars. I can find the total simply by crossing out the 2 cars from the 4 cars. There are 2 cars left.

(page 64)

My Big Fun 1st Grade Workbook

1. Read

I like to split the adding numbers into numbers that are easier to work with. I can show my favorite strategy. T = tens, O = ones.

Step 1. Let's add 12 and 15.

T O	T O
12 + 15 = ___	

Step 2. Add the tens together.

T O	T O	T O
10 + 10 = 20		

Step 3. Add the ones together.

T O	T O
2 + 5 = 7	

Step 4. Add the tens and ones to find the total.

T	O	T O
20 + 7 = 27		

1. Add

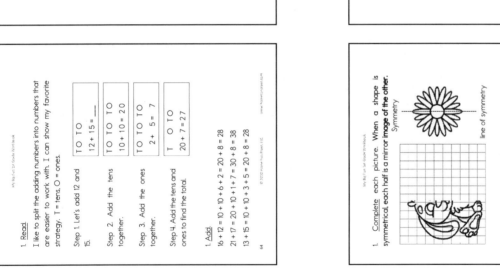

$16 + 12 = 10 + 10 + 6 + 2 = 20 + 8 = 28$

$21 + 17 = 20 + 10 + 1 + 7 = 30 + 8 = 38$

$13 + 15 = 10 + 10 + 3 + 5 = 20 + 8 = 28$

(page 68)

My Big Fun 1st Grade Workbook

1. Complete each picture. When a shape is symmetrical, each half is a mirror image of the other.

Symmetry

line of symmetry

2. Add

$$\begin{array}{r}1\\+7\\\hline8\end{array}\qquad\begin{array}{r}2\\+5\\\hline7\end{array}\qquad\begin{array}{r}3\\+3\\\hline6\end{array}\qquad\begin{array}{r}6\\+2\\\hline\end{array}\qquad\begin{array}{r}4\\+1\\\hline5\end{array}$$

$$\begin{array}{r}2\\+6\\\hline8\end{array}\qquad\begin{array}{r}1\\+5\\\hline6\end{array}\qquad\begin{array}{r}3\\+2\\\hline\end{array}\qquad\begin{array}{r}5\\+4\\\hline\end{array}\qquad\begin{array}{r}8\\+1\\\hline\end{array}$$

(page 63)

My Big Fun 1st Grade Workbook

1. Add Use a number line to show the jumps.

$2 + 7 = 9$

0 1 2 3 4 5 6 7 8 9 10

$6 + 4 = 10$

0 1 2 3 4 5 6 7 8 9 10

$9 + 1 = 10$

0 1 2 3 4 5 6 7 8 9 10

$50 + 50 = 100$

0 10 20 30 40 50 60 70 80 90 100

$40 + 40 = 80$

0 10 20 30 40 50 60 70 80 90 100

$30 + 70 = 100$

0 10 20 30 40 50 60 70 80 90 100

(page 67)

My Big Fun 1st Grade Workbook

1. Use cupcakes to make '10. Color the cupcakes brown and yellow.

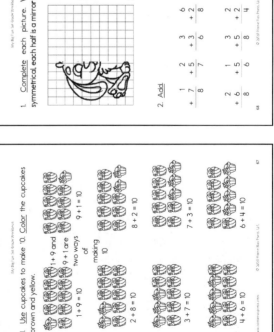

$1 + 9 = 10$

1 + 9 and 9 + 1 are two ways of making 10

$2 + 8 = 10$

$3 + 7 = 10$

$4 + 6 = 10$

$9 + 1 = 10$

$8 + 2 = 10$

$7 + 3 = 10$

$6 + 4 = 10$

1. Subtract:

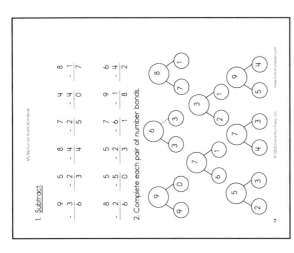

9	5	8	7	4	8
− 3	− 2	− 4	− 2	− 0	− 1
6	3	4	5	4	7

8	5	5	7	9	6
− 2	− 0	− 2	− 6	− 1	− 4
6	5	3	1	8	2

2. Complete each pair of number bonds.

74

I can subtract numbers using column subtraction.
Hint: Write ones under ones. Write tens under tens.

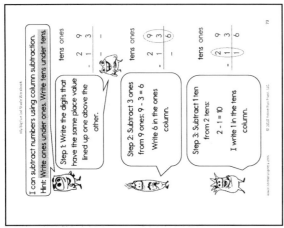

tens ones
2 9
− 1 3

Step 1: Write the digits that have the same place value lined up one above the other.

Step 2: Subtract 3 ones from 9 ones: 9 − 3 = 6. Write 6 in the ones column.

Step 3: Subtract 1 ten from 2 tens: 2 − 1 = 1. I write 1 in the tens column.

73

---

1. Read

I like to split the numbers I subtract into numbers that are easier to work with. I can show my favorite strategy.

Step 1: Let's subtract 13 from 38. → 38 − 13 = ___

Step 2: Subtract the tens from 38. → 38 − 10 = 28

Step 3: Subtract the ones from the remaining 38. → 38 − 3 = 35

1. Subtract.

5 − 1 = 4	6 − 1 = 5	9 − 1 = 8
8 − 2 = 6	4 − 2 = 2	7 − 2 = 5
3 − 3 = 0	6 − 3 = 3	8 − 3 = 5
7 − 4 = 3	9 − 4 = 5	5 − 4 = 1

72

---

1. Subtract. Use a number line to show the jumps.

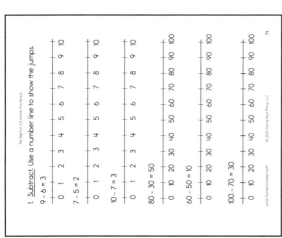

9 − 6 = 3

7 − 5 = 2

10 − 7 = 3

80 − 30 = 50

60 − 50 = 10

100 − 70 = 30

71

---

1. Color the flowers with the smaller number in each group.

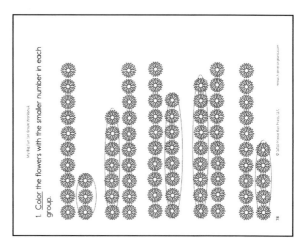

78

---

1. Subtract.

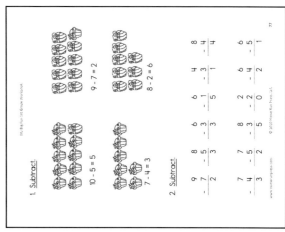

10 − 5 = 5   9 − 7 = 2   8 − 2 = 6

7 − 4 = 3

2. Subtract.

77

---

1. If 5 cupcakes are eaten, how many are left?   10 − 5 = 5

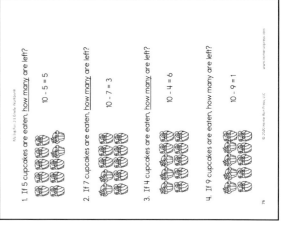

2. If 7 cupcakes are eaten, how many are left?   10 − 7 = 3

3. If 4 cupcakes are eaten, how many are left?   10 − 4 = 6

4. If 9 cupcakes are eaten, how many are left?   10 − 9 = 1

76

---

1. Subtract.

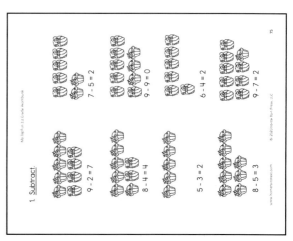

9 − 2 = 7   7 − 5 = 2

8 − 4 = 4   9 − 9 = 0

5 − 3 = 2   6 − 4 = 2

8 − 5 = 3   9 − 7 = 2

75

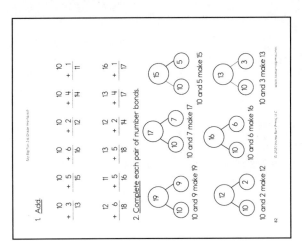

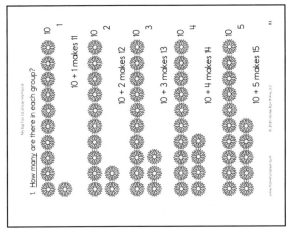

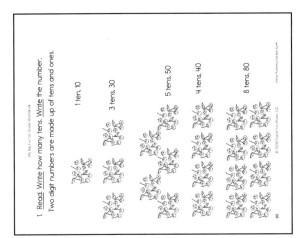

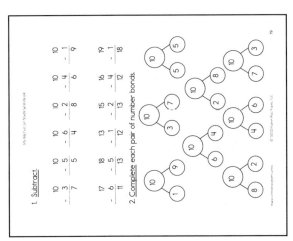

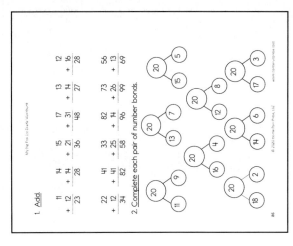

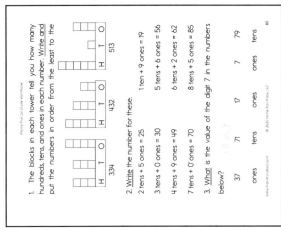

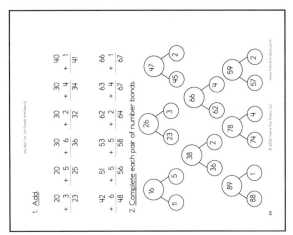

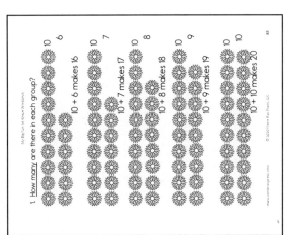

Page 87

1. Subtract.

25	28	37	33	37	42
- 3	- 5	- 6	- 2	- 4	- 1
22	23	31	31	33	41

47	56	58	67	69	66
- 4	- 5	- 5	- 2	- 4	- 5
43	51	53	65	65	61

2. Complete each pair of number bonds.

Page 88

1. Subtract.

34	28	45	37	57	47
- 12	- 14	- 21	- 31	- 14	- 16
22	14	24	6	43	31

22	64	57	39	48	33
- 10	- 41	- 25	- 14	- 26	- 11
12	23	32	25	22	22

2. Complete each pair of number bonds.

Page 89

1. How many more do I need to add to the second group to make each group the same?

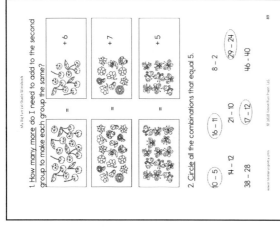

+ 6

+ 7

+ 5

2. Circle all the combinations that equal 5.

10 - 5	16 - 11	8 - 2
14 - 12	21 - 10	29 - 24
38 - 28	17 - 12	46 - 40

Page 90

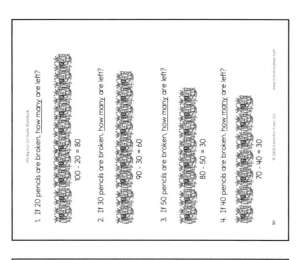

1. If 20 pencils are broken, how many are left?

100 - 20 = 80

2. If 30 pencils are broken, how many are left?

90 - 30 = 60

3. If 50 pencils are broken, how many are left?

80 - 50 = 30

4. If 40 pencils are broken, how many are left?

70 - 40 = 30

Page 91

1. Read. Write how many tens. Write the number.

Three digit numbers are made up of hundreds, tens, and ones.

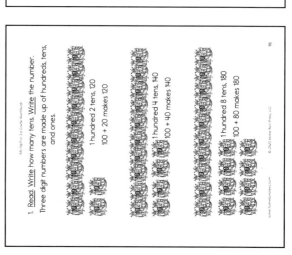

1 hundred 2 tens, 120
100 + 20 makes 120

1 hundred 4 tens, 140
100 + 40 makes 140

1 hundred 8 tens, 180
100 + 80 makes 180

Page 92

1. Add.

100	100	100	100	100	100
+ 25	+ 15	+ 46	+ 12	+ 47	+ 71
125	115	146	112	147	171

120	110	130	120	130	160
+ 6	+ 5	+ 5	+ 4	+ 4	+ 1
126	115	135	122	134	161

2. Complete each pair of number bonds.

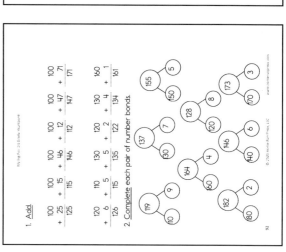

Page 93

1. Read.

Place value is the amount a digit is worth in a number.

Hundreds	Tens	Ones
2	6	3

2 hundreds = the value of 2 in this number is 200

6 tens = the value of 6 in this number is 60

3 ones = the value of 3 in this number is 3

```
  4 0 0
    6 0
      3
+ -----
  4 6 3
```

```
  6 0 0
    1 0
      5
+ -----
  6 1 5
```

Page 94

1. What is the value of the 4 in each of these numbers? Circle the right answer.

416	a) Hundreds	b) Tens	c) Ones
974	a) Hundreds	b) Tens	c) Ones
416	a) Hundreds	b) Tens	c) Ones
245	a) Hundreds	b) Tens	c) Ones
624	a) Hundreds	b) Tens	c) Ones

2. Complete each addition number sentence with tens and ones. The first one is done for you.

45 = 40 + 5	61 = 60 + 1	19 = 10 + 9
30 = 30 + 0	74 = 70 + 4	37 = 30 + 7
52 = 50 + 2	65 = 60 + 5	58 = 50 + 8
98 = 90 + 8	87 = 80 + 7	60 = 60 + 0

Page 95

1. Write the missing numbers.

50 + 3 = 53	800 + 0 + 7 = 807
20 + 5 = 25	300 + 20 + 8 = 328
90 + 6 = 96	900 + 70 + 2 = 972
60 + 2 = 62	400 + 30 + 0 = 430
10 + 9 = 19	200 + 40 + 4 = 244
40 + 8 = 48	500 + 90 + 5 = 595

2. Circle the correct answer.

I have a series of numbers: 0, 2, 4, 6, 8. What is the next number?

a) 10   (b) 8   c) 12   d) 7

95

Page 96

1. Circle the correct answer.

I have a series of numbers: 1, 2, 4, 7. What is the next number?

(a) 7   b) 8   c) 9   d) 10

2. Color the 2nd frog green. Color the 3rd frog brown. Color the 5th frog black. Color the 6th frog grey.

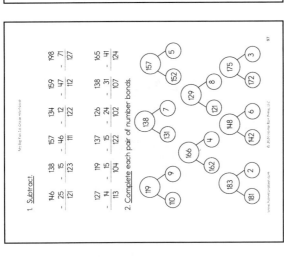

3. Write the missing numbers.

400 + 60 + 8 = 468	500 + 0 + 9 = 509
100 + 30 + 5 = 135	600 + 80 + 3 = 683
200 + 40 + 5 = 245	200 + 40 + 8 = 248
600 + 20 + 1 = 621	700 + 90 + 1 = 791

96

Page 97

1. Subtract.

146	138	157	134	159	198
-25	-15	-46	-12	-47	-71
121	123	111	122	112	127

127	119	137	126	138	165
-14	-15	-15	-24	-31	-41
113	104	122	102	107	124

2. Complete each pair of number bonds.

97

Page 98

1. Read.

I often need to know if a number is the same as, smaller than, or larger than another number. My teacher calls this comparing numbers. Look at these candles. There are six candles in each row. My candles says that the number in one row is equal to the number in the second row. 6 = 6

My sister has six candles in the top row and three candles in the bottom row. She says the number in the top row is greater than the number in the bottom row. 6 > 3.   6 is greater than 3.

98

Page 99

1. Read.

My brother has five candles in the top row and six candles in the bottom row. He says the number in the top row is less than the number in the second row. 5 < 6.   5 is less than 6.

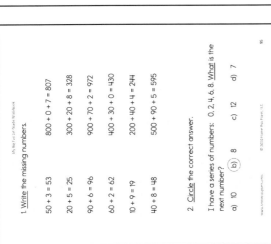

2. Circle the missing number from the choice box to make the inequality true.

5 < ___ < 9
a) 4   b) 0   c) 6

9 < ___ < 11
a) 7   b) 1   c) 10

15 < ___ < 25
a) 11   b) 20   c) 35

76 < ___ < 90
a) 89   b) 71   c) 100

99

Page 100

1. Read.

When I round, I change a number to another number that is almost the same in value, but it is easier to work with.

For digits 0, 1, 2, and 4, we round down   For digits 5, 6, 7, 8, and 9, we round up

0 1 2 3 4 5 6 7 8 9 10

Look at 52. We look at the ones digit. It's 2.

50 51 52 53 54 55 56 57 58 59 60

We round down to 50.

Now, look at 58. The ones digit is 8.

50 51 52 53 54 55 56 57 58 59 60

So we round UP to 60.

100

Page 101

1. Which is more? Compare the numbers using ">", "<", or "=".

3 ones < 2 tens	10 ones = 1 ten
3 tens > 8 ones	2 tens > 1 ten

4 tens 2 ones < 41 ones
1 ten 2 ones < 1 ten 20 ones
2 tens and 3 ones < 3 tens and 2 ones

2. Round each number to the nearest 10. Look at the next digit to the right. If it is 0, 1, 2, 3, or 4, then ROUND DOWN. If it is 5, 6, 7, 8, 9, then ROUND UP.

6	10	8	10	5	10
13	10	19	20	16	20
11	10	17	20	19	20
22	20	25	30	23	20
28	30	24	20	29	30

101

Page 102

1. Which is more? Write the missing numbers to make the comparison true. Answers may vary.

12 ones > 8 ones	7 ones > 1 ten
1 ten = 10 ones	2 tens = 20 ones
5 ones > 3 ones	12 ones < 2 tens

15 ones < 1 ten 6 ones
1 ten 8 ones > 1 ten 5 ones
3 tens and 3 ones = 2 tens and 13 ones

2. Round each number to the nearest 100. Look at the next digit to the right. If it is 0, 1, 2, 3, or 4, then ROUND DOWN. If it is 5, 6, 7, 8, 9, then ROUND UP.

153	200	208	200	75	700
913	900	259	300	246	200
371	400	557	600	469	500
622	600	485	500	923	900

102

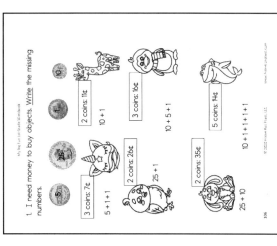

My Big Fun 1st Grade Workbook

1. I need money to buy objects. <u>Write the missing numbers.</u>

2 coins: 11¢
10 + 1

3 coins: 16¢
10 + 5 + 1

3 coins: 7¢
5 + 1 + 1

2 coins: 26¢
25 + 1

2 coins: 35¢
25 + 10

5 coins: 14¢
10 + 1 + 1 + 1 + 1

106

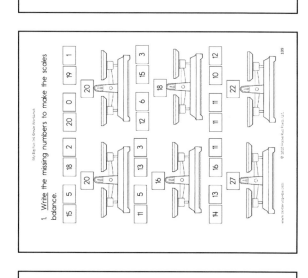

My Big Fun 1st Grade Workbook

1. My Grandma baked 2 pumpkin pies. I ate a half of the total amount of pies. How many pie(s) are left?

<u>Circle your answer:</u>
0 ① 2 3 4 5

A half is one of two equal parts of one whole. If two pies are one whole, I could eat 1 pie which is a half. Another half is left. So, I circle 1.

I found 4 shells. My sister broke a half of the shells. Color these shells red. How many shells are left?

<u>Circle your answer:</u>
0 1 ② 3 4 5

I got 6 cupcakes. I ate a half of them. Color the cupcakes I ate. How many cupcakes are left?

<u>Circle your answer:</u>
0 1 2 ③ 4 5

110

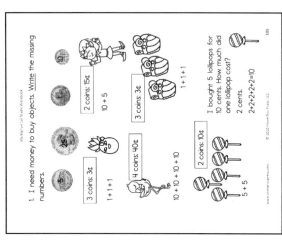

My Big Fun 1st Grade Workbook

1. I need money to buy objects. <u>Write the missing numbers.</u>

2 coins: 15¢
10 + 5

3 coins: 3¢
1 + 1 + 1

3 coins: 3¢
1 + 1 + 1

4 coins: 40¢
10 + 10 + 10 + 10

2 coins: 10¢
5 + 5

I bought 5 lollipops for 10 cents. How much did one lollipop cost?
2 cents.
2+2+2+2+2=10

105

My Big Fun 1st Grade Workbook

1. Write the missing numbers to make the scales balance.

109

My Big Fun 1st Grade Workbook

1. Read

I have tons of candies. I need to estimate because it would take too long to count the exact number. I count 5 candies in the bottom row. There are 4 rows, so I can say there are about 5 + 5 + 5 + 5 candies, which is 20 candies.

column

row

I often don't need to count the candies exactly. If I have two bags of candies that cost the same, I will get the bag with more candies.

$1

104

My Big Fun 1st Grade Workbook

1. Write the missing numbers to make the scales balance.

108

My Big Fun 1st Grade Workbook

1. Read

Even numbers are made of pairs.

An odd number is always 1 more or 1 less than an even number.

Even numbers end with a digit of 0, 2, 4, 6, 8.
Odd numbers end with a digit of 1, 3, 5, 7, 9.

2. Underline the even numbers.

1, 2, 3, 4, 5, 6, 7, 8, 9, 10, 11, 12, 13, 14, 15, 16

3. Circle the odd numbers.

⑮, 16, ⑰, 18, ⑲, 20, ㉑, 22, ㉓, 24, ㉕, 26

103

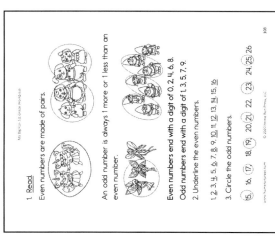

My Big Fun 1st Grade Workbook

1. I need money to buy objects. <u>Write the missing numbers.</u>

3 coins: 15¢
5 + 5 + 5

2 coins: 20¢
10 + 10

2 coins: 15¢
10 + 5

4 coins: 17¢
10 + 5 + 1 + 1

2 coins: 30¢
25 + 5

5 coins: 17¢
5 + 5 + 5 + 1 + 1

107

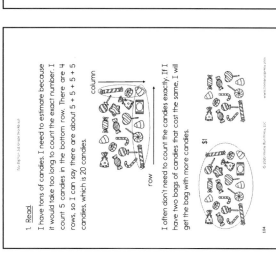

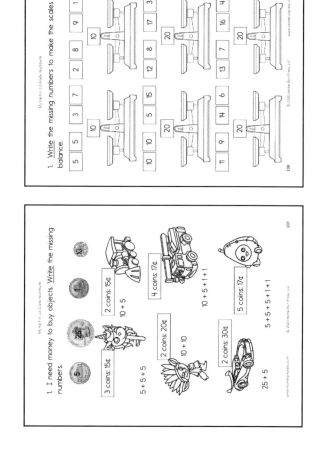

1. Shade a half for each pair.

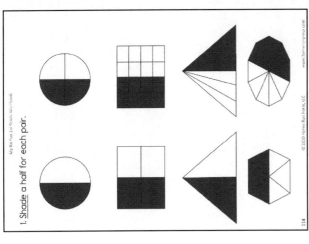

114

---

1. When you share equally between two elves, both sets of sweets and fruits have the same amount. Count how many for each elf?

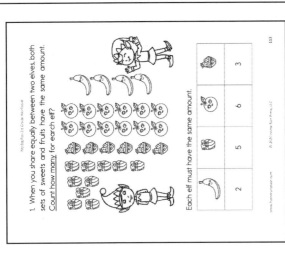

Each elf must have the same amount:

2	5	6	3

113

---

1. What number am I?

Half of me is 1 and double me is 4.

One whole:

A half of two equal parts of one whole is one:

Double means take twice as much or as many:

Half of me is 2 and double me is 8.

I am 4.

Half of me is 5 and double me is 20.

I am 10.

Half of me is 10 and double me is 40.

I am 20.

Half of me is 50 and double me is 200.

I am 100.

112

---

1. I got 8 candies. I ate a half of the candies. Color them red. How many candies are left?

Circle your answer:
0 1 2 3 (4) 5

I found 10 flowers. A half of the flowers were blooming. How many flowers were not blooming?

Circle your answer:
0 1 2 3 4 (5)

The pumpkin weighed 2 pounds. We ate a half of it. How many pounds are left?

Circle your answer:
0 (1) 2 3 4 5

My birthday cake weighed 10 pounds! My friends ate a half of the cake. How many pounds are left?

Circle your answer: 0 1 2 3 4 (5)

111

---

1. Draw the minute and hour hands to show the time.

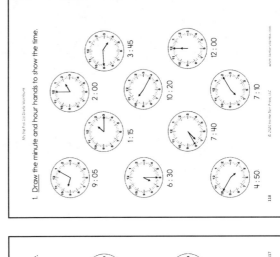

3:45   12:00

2:00   10:20   7:10

1:15   7:40

9:05   6:30   4:50

118

---

1. Draw the minute and hour hands to show the time.

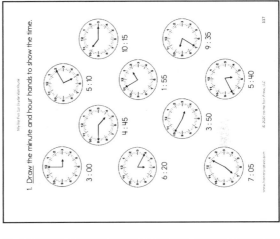

10:15   9:35

5:10   5:40

4:45   1:55

3:50

3:00   3:00...

6:20   5:40

7:05   7:05

117

The minute hand is the long hand. It moves 60 minutes. It points to the 12 to show the hour's time.

As the minute hand moves around the clock, the hour hand moves from one hour to the next. The hour hand is the short hand. It points to the hour number.

Read: two thirty
or thirty minutes after two
or thirty minutes before three

Write: 2:30

60 minutes = 1 hour

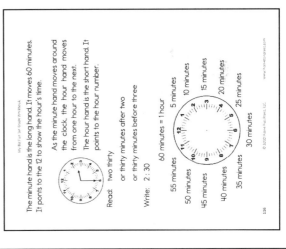

5 minutes
10 minutes
15 minutes
20 minutes
25 minutes
30 minutes
35 minutes
40 minutes
45 minutes
50 minutes
55 minutes

116

---

1. Shade one part out of 8 equal parts.

Shade two parts out of 4 equal parts.

Shade five parts out of 6 equal parts.

Shade seven parts out of 10 equal parts.

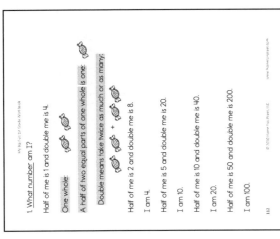

115

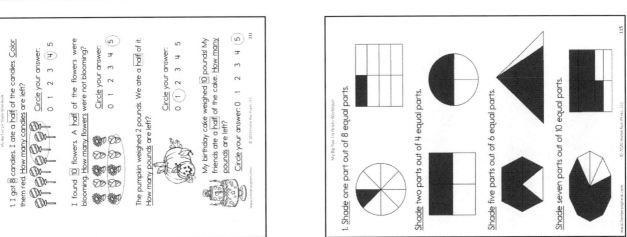

1. I am building a solid slab of rocks: the two rocks next to each other are added to get the number up above. Fill in the missing numbers.

11
5	6
2	3	3
1	2	2	1

2. Write the numbers in order, from the smallest to the largest.

7, 9, 3, 1, 2, 11, 5, 12, 8, 4, 0, 10, 6

0, 1, 2, 3, 4, 5, 6, 7, 8, 9, 10, 11, 12

3. Complements to 10. Circle the missing numbers from the choice box to make the equations true.

11 + 9 = 20   a) 8   b) 7   c) 9

5 + 15 = 20   a) 10   b) 5   c) 15

7 + 13 = 20   a) 13   b) 1   c) 4

14 + 6 = 20   a) 4   b) 16   c) 6

---

1. Circle the right answer.

30 + 25 = 55   a) 25   b) 30   c) 35

2. Complements to 100. Circle the missing numbers from the choice box to make the equations true.

50 + ___ = 100   a) 35   b) 50   c) 60

90 + ___ = 100   a) 10   b) 100   c) 20

20 + ___ = 100   a) 60   b) 20   c) 80

3. Circle the right answer:

I have a series of numbers: 3, 6, 9, 12, ___

What is the next number?

A) 13   B) 15   C) 18   D) 14

4. I have some numbers and signs: 1, 5, 3, +, -.

Write the equation that equals one of the answer choices.

5 + 3 - 1 = 7

A) 10   B) 7   C) 4   D) 9

---

1. Solve the problem:

1047: the sum of the ones and hundreds is 7 + 0 = 7.   A) 5   B) 8   C) 7

2. I start at 0 and count on in twos. Will I say 11? 0, 2, 4, 6, 8, 10, 12

Why? 11 is an odd number.

I start at 0 and count on in twos. Will I say 16? 0, 2, 4, 6, 8, 10, 12, 14, 16

Why? 16 is an even number.

3. Find the value.

853:

The sum of the ones and tens is 3 + 5 = 8.

The difference between the hundreds and tens is 8 - 5 = 3.

The difference between the hundreds and ones is 8 - 3 = 5.

---

1. Solve the problems:

I had 8 candies. I gave 4 of them to my sister. How many candies has I left?   8 - 4 = 4 (candies)

There are 10 kids at a playground. I counted 7 boys. How many girls are there?   3 girls.

10 - 7 = 3 (girls)

My brother bought 11 chocolate cupcakes and 5 vanilla cupcakes. How many cupcakes did he buy in all?   16 cupcakes.

11 + 5 = 16 (cupcakes)

I found 6 easter eggs. My sister found 4 more Easter eggs than I did. My brother found 7 less Easter eggs than my sister. How many Easter eggs did my brother find?   3 Easter eggs.

6 + 4 = 10 (sister)   10 - 7 = 3 (brother)

---

1. Solve the problems:

I had 15 cupcakes. I ate some cupcakes, and I had 12 cupcakes left. How many cupcakes did I eat?

3 cupcakes: 15 - 12 = 3

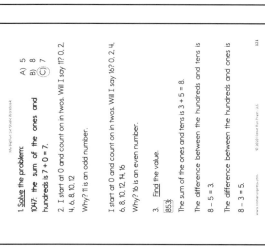

My brother has 18 trucks and race cars. 3 of them are trucks. How many race cars does he have?

15 race cars: 18 - 3 = 15

My sister saw 11 butterflies. My brother saw 4 butterflies more than my sister. How many butterflies did they see altogether?

26 butterflies: 11 + 11 + 4 = 26

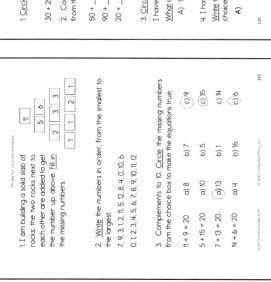

---

1. Solve the problems:

I had some cupcakes. I ate 3 cupcakes and I gave 4 cupcakes to my friend. I have 11 cupcakes left. How many cupcakes did I have at first?

18 cupcakes: 3 + 4 + 11 = 18

I had 5 yellow balloons and 5 more red balloons than yellow balloons. My friend had 8 more balloons than I had. How many balloons did my friend have?

18 balloons: 5 + 5 + 8 = 18

There are 8 oranges in a basket. My mother puts 10 small pears and 3 bananas into the basket. How many fruits are there in the basket altogether?

19 fruits: 6 + 10 + 3 = 19

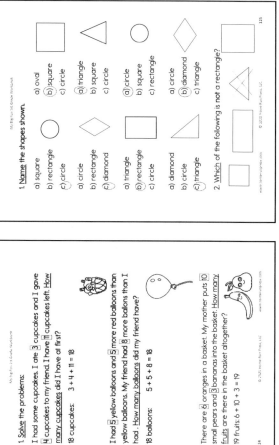

---

1. Name the shapes shown.

a) square   b) rectangle   c) circle

a) circle   b) rectangle   c) diamond

a) triangle   b) rectangle   c) circle

a) diamond   b) circle   c) triangle

a) oval   b) square   c) circle

a) triangle   b) square   c) circle

a) circle   b) square   c) rectangle

a) circle   b) diamond   c) triangle

2. Which of the following is not a rectangle?

---

1. Name the shapes shown.

a) square   b) rectangle   c) circle

a) circle   b) rectangle   c) diamond

a) square   b) rectangle   c) circle

a) diamond   b) star   c) triangle

a) oval   b) square   c) circle

a) triangle   b) square   c) circle

a) circle   b) triangle   c) rectangle

a) heart   b) diamond   c) triangle

2. Which of the following is not a triangle?

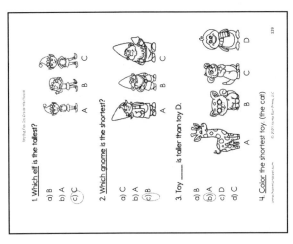

1. Which elf is the tallest?

a) B
b) A
c) C

2. Which gnome is the shortest?

a) C
b) A
c) B

3. Toy _____ is taller than toy D.

a) B
b) A
c) D
d) C

4. Color the shortest toy. (the cat)

129

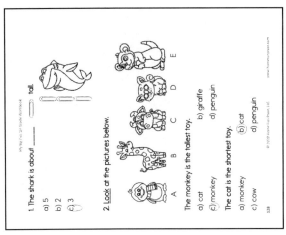

1. The shark is about _____ tall.

a) 5
b) 2
c) 3

2. Look at the pictures below.

A   B   C   D   E

The monkey is the tallest toy.

a) cat   b) giraffe
c) monkey   d) penguin

The cat is the shortest toy.

a) monkey   b) cat
c) cow   d) penguin

128

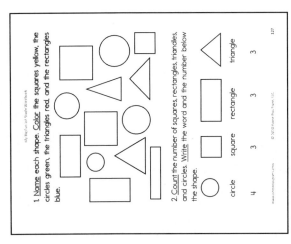

1. Name each shape. Color the squares yellow, the circles green, the triangles red, and the rectangles blue.

2. Count the number of squares, rectangles, triangles, and circles. Write the word and the number below the shape.

circle   square   rectangle   triangle

4   3   3   3

127

145

Made in the USA
Middletown, DE
22 May 2020